IN ASSOCIATION WITH

Hodder Gibson
Model Practice Papers
...SWERS

...ecimen Paper &
...r With Answers

...ational 5
...skills
...atics

...Question Paper,
...rs & 2014 Exam

HODDER
GIBSON
AN HACHETTE UK COMPANY

This book contains the official 2013 SQA Specimen Question Paper and 2014 Exam for National 5 Lifeskills Mathematics, with associated SQA approved answers modified from the official marking instructions that accompany the paper.

In addition the book contains model practice papers, together with answers, plus study skills advice. These papers, some of which may include a limited number of previously published SQA questions, have been specially commissioned by Hodder Gibson, and have been written by experienced senior teachers and examiners in line with the new National 5 syllabus and assessment outlines, Spring 2013. This is not SQA material but has been devised to provide further practice for National 5 examinations in 2014 and beyond.

Hodder Gibson is grateful to the copyright holders, as credited on the final page of the Answer Section, for permission to use their material. Every effort has been made to trace the copyright holders and to obtain their permission for the use of copyright material. Hodder Gibson will be happy to receive information allowing us to rectify any error or omission in future editions.

Hachette UK's policy is to use papers that are natural, renewable and recyclable products and made from wood grown in sustainable forests. The logging and manufacturing processes are expected to conform to the environmental regulations of the country of origin.

Orders: please contact Bookpoint Ltd, 130 Park Drive, Abingdon, Oxon OX14 4SE. Telephone: (44) 01235 827720. Fax: (44) 01235 400454. Lines are open 9.00–5.00, Monday to Saturday, with a 24-hour message answering service. Visit our website at www.hoddereducation.co.uk. Hodder Gibson can be contacted direct on: Tel: 0141 848 1609; Fax: 0141 889 6315; email: hoddergibson@hodder.co.uk

This collection first published in 2014 by
Hodder Gibson, an imprint of Hodder Education,
An Hachette UK Company
2a Christie Street
Paisley PA1 1NB

BrightRED Hodder Gibson is grateful to Bright Red Publishing Ltd for collaborative work in preparation of this book and all SQA Past Paper, National 5 and Higher for CfE Model Paper titles 2014.

Specimen Question Paper © Scottish Qualifications Authority. Answers, Model Question Papers, and Study Skills Section © Hodder Gibson. Model Question Papers creation/compilation, Answers and Study Skills section © Mike Smith. All rights reserved. Apart from any use permitted under UK copyright law, no part of this publication may be reproduced or transmitted in any form or by any means, electronic or mechanical, including photocopying and recording, or held within any information storage and retrieval system, without permission in writing from the publisher or under licence from the Copyright Licensing Agency Limited. Further details of such licences (for reprographic reproduction) may be obtained from the Copyright Licensing Agency Limited, Saffron House, 6–10 Kirby Street, London EC1N 8TS.

Typeset by PDQ Digital Media Solutions Ltd, Bungay, Suffolk NR35 1BY

Printed in the UK

A catalogue record for this title is available from the British Library

ISBN: 978-1-4718-3708-1

3 2

2015

Introduction

Study Skills – what you need to know to pass exams!

Pause for thought

Many students might skip quickly through a page like this. After all, we all know how to revise. Do you really though?

Think about this:

"IF YOU ALWAYS DO WHAT YOU ALWAYS DO, YOU WILL ALWAYS GET WHAT YOU HAVE ALWAYS GOT."

Do you like the grades you get? Do you want to do better? If you get full marks in your assessment, then that's great! Change nothing! This section is just to help you get that little bit better than you already are.

There are two main parts to the advice on offer here. The first part highlights fairly obvious things but which are also very important. The second part makes suggestions about revision that you might not have thought about but which WILL help you.

Part 1

DOH! It's so obvious but …

Start revising in good time

Don't leave it until the last minute – this will make you panic.

Make a revision timetable that sets out work time AND play time.

Sleep and eat!

Obvious really, and very helpful. Avoid arguments or stressful things too – even games that wind you up. You need to be fit, awake and focused!

Know your place!

Make sure you know exactly **WHEN and WHERE** your exams are.

Know your enemy!

Make sure you know what to expect in the exam.

How is the paper structured?

How much time is there for each question?

What types of question are involved?

Which topics seem to come up time and time again?

Which topics are your strongest and which are your weakest?

Are all topics compulsory or are there choices?

Learn by DOING!

There is no substitute for past papers and practice papers – they are simply essential! Tackling this collection of papers and answers is exactly the right thing to be doing as your exams approach.

Part 2

People learn in different ways. Some like low light, some bright. Some like early morning, some like evening / night. Some prefer warm, some prefer cold. But everyone uses their BRAIN and the brain works when it is active. Passive learning – sitting gazing at notes – is the most INEFFICIENT way to learn anything. Below you will find tips and ideas for making your revision more effective and maybe even more enjoyable. What follows gets your brain active, and active learning works!

Activity 1 – Stop and review

Step 1

When you have done no more than 5 minutes of revision reading STOP!

Step 2

Write a heading in your own words which sums up the topic you have been revising.

Step 3

Write a summary of what you have revised in no more than two sentences. Don't fool yourself by saying, "I know it, but I cannot put it into words". That just means you don't know it well enough. If you cannot write your summary, revise that section again, knowing that you must write a summary at the end of it. Many of you will have notebooks full of blue/black ink writing. Many of the pages will not be especially attractive or memorable so try to liven them up a bit with colour as you are reviewing and rewriting. **This is a great memory aid, and memory is the most important thing.**

Activity 2 — Use technology!

Why should everything be written down? Have you thought about "mental" maps, diagrams, cartoons and colour to help you learn? And rather than write down notes, why not record your revision material?

What about having a text message revision session with friends? Keep in touch with them to find out how and what they are revising and share ideas and questions.

Why not make a video diary where you tell the camera what you are doing, what you think you have learned and what you still have to do? No one has to see or hear it, but the process of having to organise your thoughts in a formal way to explain something is a very important learning practice.

Be sure to make use of electronic files. You could begin to summarise your class notes. Your typing might be slow, but it will get faster and the typed notes will be easier to read than the scribbles in your class notes. Try to add different fonts and colours to make your work stand out. You can easily Google relevant pictures, cartoons and diagrams which you can copy and paste to make your work more attractive and **MEMORABLE**.

Activity 3 – This is it. Do this and you will know lots!

Step 1

In this task you must be very honest with yourself! Find the SQA syllabus for your subject (www.sqa.org.uk). Look at how it is broken down into main topics called MANDATORY knowledge. That means stuff you MUST know.

Step 2

BEFORE you do ANY revision on this topic, write a list of everything that you already know about the subject. It might be quite a long list but you only need to write it once. It shows you all the information that is already in your long-term memory so you know what parts you do not need to revise!

Step 3

Pick a chapter or section from your book or revision notes. Choose a fairly large section or a whole chapter to get the most out of this activity.

With a buddy, use Skype, Facetime, Twitter or any other communication you have, to play the game "If this is the answer, what is the question?". For example, if you are revising Geography and the answer you provide is "meander", your buddy would have to make up a question like "What is the word that describes a feature of a river where it flows slowly and bends often from side to side?".

Make up 10 "answers" based on the content of the chapter or section you are using. Give this to your buddy to solve while you solve theirs.

Step 4

Construct a wordsearch of at least 10 X 10 squares. You can make it as big as you like but keep it realistic. Work together with a group of friends. Many apps allow you to make wordsearch puzzles online. The words and phrases can go in any direction and phrases can be split. Your puzzle must only contain facts linked to the topic you are revising. Your task is to find 10 bits of information to hide in your puzzle, but you must not repeat information that you used in Step 3. DO NOT show where the words are. Fill up empty squares with random letters. Remember to keep a note of where your answers are hidden but do not show your friends. When you have a complete puzzle, exchange it with a friend to solve each other's puzzle.

Step 5

Now make up 10 questions (not "answers" this time) based on the same chapter used in the previous two tasks. Again, you must find NEW information that you have not yet used. Now it's getting hard to find that new information! Again, give your questions to a friend to answer.

Step 6

As you have been doing the puzzles, your brain has been actively searching for new information. Now write a NEW LIST that contains only the new information you have discovered when doing the puzzles. Your new list is the one to look at repeatedly for short bursts over the next few days. Try to remember more and more of it without looking at it. After a few days, you should be able to add words from your second list to your first list as you increase the information in your long-term memory.

FINALLY! Be inspired...

Make a list of different revision ideas and beside each one write **THINGS I HAVE** tried, **THINGS I WILL** try and **THINGS I MIGHT** try. Don't be scared of trying something new.

And remember – "FAIL TO PREPARE AND PREPARE TO FAIL!"

National 5 Lifeskills Mathematics

The course

The Lifeskills Mathematics course is a new qualification which focuses on the application of mathematical skills in real-life contexts.

The National 5 Lifeskills Mathematics course aims to enable you to develop:

- a range of mathematical techniques and apply these to real-life problems or situations
- the ability to analyse a range of real-life problems or situations
- a confident and independent approach towards the use of mathematics in real-life situations
- the ability to select, apply and combine mathematical skills to new or unfamiliar situations in life and work
- the ability to use mathematical reasoning skills to generalise, support arguments, draw conclusions, assess risk and make informed decisions
- the ability to analyse, interpret and present a range of information
- the ability to communicate mathematical information in a variety of forms
- the ability to think creatively and in abstract ways.

Before starting this course you should already have the knowledge, understanding and skills required to achieve a pass in National 4 Lifeskills Mathematics and/or be proficient in appropriate experiences and outcomes.

This course enables you to further develop your knowledge, understanding, skills and reasoning processes in personal finance, statistics, geometry, measure, numeracy and data. The table outlines the topics covered in each area of the course:

Finance	Statistics	Numeracy
Budgeting	Investigate probability/risk	Select and use appropriate
Income and pay slips	Statistical diagrams	notation and units
Tax and deductions	Analyse/compare data sets	Select and carry out operations
Best deal	Line of best fit	including:
Currency conversion		• working to given decimal places
Interest rates and saving/borrowing		• rounding to given significant figures
Geometry	**Graphical Data**	• fractions and mixed numbers
Gradient	Extract/interpret data	• percentages, including compound
Composite shapes: Area	from at least three different	• speed, distance, time
Composite solids: Volume	graphical forms	• area
Pythagoras' theorem	Make/justify decisions based	• volume
Measure	on interpretation of data	• ratio
Scale drawing	Make/justify decisions based	• proportion, direct and indirect
Bearings	on probability	
Container packing		
Precedence tables		
Time management		
Tolerance		

You will use your reasoning skills and the skills above, linked to real-life contexts. The amount of reasoning is what makes Lifeskills Mathematics different. You will be asked to analyse, compare, justify and communicate information.

Assessment

To gain the course award, you must pass the three Units – Managing Finance and Statistics, Geometry and Measures and Numeracy and Data – as well as the examination. The Units are assessed internally on a pass/fail basis and the examination is set and marked externally by SQA. It tests skills beyond the minimum competence required for the Units.

The number of marks and the times allotted for the examination papers are as follows:

Paper 1 (non-calculator)   35 marks   50 minutes

Paper 2   55 marks   1 hour 40 minutes

The course award is graded A–D, the grade being determined by the total mark you score in the examination.

The papers are "structured" which means that you write your answer on the exam paper next to the question. This gives you the advantage of being able to complete tables, draw on graphs and annotate diagrams, without having to draw them yourself.

Some tips for achieving a good mark

- **DOING** maths questions is the most effective use of your study time. You will benefit much more from spending 30 minutes doing maths questions than spending several hours copying out notes or reading a maths textbook.

- Practise doing the types of questions that are likely to appear in the exam. Use the marking instructions to check your answers and to understand what the examiners are looking for. Ask your teacher for help if you get stuck.

- **SHOW ALL WORKING CLEARLY.** The instructions on the front of the exam paper state that *"Full credit will only be given where the solution contains appropriate working"*. A "correct" answer with no working may only be awarded partial marks or even no marks at all. An incomplete answer will be awarded marks for any appropriate working. Attempt every question, even if you are not sure whether you are correct or not. Your solution may contain working which will gain some marks. A blank response is certain to be awarded no marks. Never score out working unless you have something better to replace it with.

- Reasoning skills are a major part of Lifeskills Mathematics. One way of showing your reasoning process is by showing all of your working. Quite often you will be asked to *"Use your working to justify your answer"* – so you cannot just say "yes" or "no" without your working.

- Communication is very important in presenting solutions to questions. Diagrams are often a good way of conveying information and enabling markers to understand your working. Where a diagram is included in a . question, it is often good practice to mark in any dimensions etc, which you work out and may use later.

- In Paper 1, you have to carry out calculations without a calculator. Ensure that you practise your number skills regularly, especially within questions that test course content. Also make sure that after you have calculated an answer you state the **units**, if appropriate. Paper 1 will be a mixture of short, medium and extended questions covering a single "skill", to three or four skills across the Units.

- In Paper 2, you will be allowed to use a calculator. Always use **your own** calculator. Different calculators often function in slightly different ways, so make sure that you know how to operate yours. Having to use a calculator that you are unfamiliar with on the day of the exam may cause frustration and loss of time. Paper 2 will be a mixture of short, medium and extended **case studies**. These will follow a "theme" and can cover one skill within a Unit to three or more from across the Units.

- Prepare thoroughly to tackle questions from **all** parts of the course. Always try all parts of a question. Just because you could not complete part (a), for example, this does not mean you could not do part (b) or (c).

- Look at how many **marks** are allocated to a question – this will give you an idea of how much work is required. The more marks, the more work!

- Look for **key words** in questions: state, calculate, compare, plot, sketch, draw, justify.

Some areas to consider

Each question is likely to have a mixture of strategy, process and communication marks.

You will be expected to:

- select a strategy (there may be more than one way to do a question)
- process the information (for example, carry out a calculation)
- communicate your answer (for example, "yes the company would accept as tolerance is within limits").

Here are some examples to consider:

Types of question	Things to consider
You may be asked to mark points on a scatter diagram, draw a line of best fit and then compare it with one already drawn.	Ensure points are **plotted accurately**. Try to make the **"slope"** of the line match points. Try to have about same number of points above and below the line of best fit.
You may be asked to make a scale drawing of, for example, a garden. You may then be asked to calculate measurements from this drawing.	Choose a scale which gives a good size, to fit the space given to you. **State the scale** you have used. Use this scale to calculate actual sizes. Remember to **state units**.
You may be asked to construct a box plot. You may have to compare this with one given.	Make sure you have a scale clearly marked. Make sure you mark in the **five-figure summary**. Valid comparison: 1 mark equals one comparison, 2 marks equal two comparison statements. For example, "plot 2 has a higher median and a greater spread".

In Paper 2 you have been given more time to allow you to read and absorb the information given.

Use the first one or two case studies to get "into the swing of it". These will be short case studies looking at perhaps only one skill, for example, from Managing Finance and Statistics you may be tasked to complete a payslip. Take your time and complete these accurately – this could be a 5 mark start to the paper!

You may be asked to calculate the standard deviation for a set of data. Again, take your time and do this accurately. These are "processing" questions and should allow you a "cushion" before you put your reasoning into place for later case studies.

A medium-length case study will cover areas such as speed, distance, time along with money. For example, "what will be the cost of fuel for a journey given the data on distance, speed, fuel consumption?" and so on. An extended case study will perhaps cover skills from across all three Units. For example, from Working to a Budget, "could you plan a holiday taking in three different places, with certain likely temperatures over a period of time, staying in the cheapest hotels and travelling by train?"

In Paper 2 you should not have to "turn pages" between information and questions. If it is a short case study, there will be space on one page. If it is a longer case study, the information will be on the left-hand page and the questions on the right-hand side, as in the diagram below.

Left-hand page	Right-hand page
Table of information	Question 1a
Statements of information	Question 1b
Facts and figures	Question 1 c
Graphs or diagrams	

Look through these model papers to get a feel for the type and variety of questions you could be asked.

Remember that Lifeskills Mathematics is all about analysing, interpreting, solving, justifying and communicating!

Good luck!

Remember that the rewards for passing National 5 Lifeskills Mathematics are well worth it! Your pass will help you get the future you want for yourself. In the exam, be confident in your own ability. If you're not sure how to answer a question, trust your instincts and just give it a go anyway. Keep calm and don't panic! GOOD LUCK!

2013 Specimen Question Paper

N5

National
Qualifications
SPECIMEN ONLY

Mark

SQ26/N5/01

Lifeskills Mathematics
Paper 1
(Non-Calculator)

Date — Not applicable

Duration — 50 minutes

Fill in these boxes and read what is printed below.

Full name of centre

Town

Forename(s)

Surname

Number of seat

Date of birth

Day	Month	Year
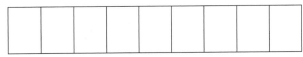		

Scottish candidate number

Total marks — 35

You may NOT use a calculator.

Attempt ALL questions.

Use **blue** or **black** ink. Pencil may be used for graphs and diagrams only.

Write your working and answers in the spaces provided. Additional space for answers is provided at the end of this booklet. If you use this space, write clearly the number of the question you are attempting.

Square-ruled paper is provided at the back of this booklet.

Full credit will be given only to solutions which contain appropriate working.

State the units for your answer where appropriate.

Before leaving the examination room you must give this booklet to the Invigilator. If you do not, you may lose all the marks for this paper.

FORMULAE LIST

Circumference of a circle: $C = \pi d$

Area of a circle: $A = \pi r^2$

Theorem of Pythagoras: 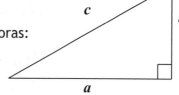 $a^2 + b^2 = c^2$

Volume of a cylinder: $V = \pi r^2 h$

Volume of a prism: $V = Ah$

Standard deviation: $s = \sqrt{\dfrac{\Sigma(x - \bar{x})^2}{n-1}} = \sqrt{\dfrac{\Sigma x^2 - (\Sigma x)^2 / n}{n-1}}$, where n is the sample size.

Gradient: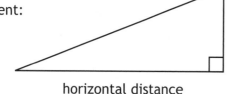

$$\text{gradient} = \frac{\text{vertical height}}{\text{horizontal distance}}$$

MARKS | DO NOT WRITE IN THIS MARGIN

Attempt ALL questions

1. Dave and Elaine each have the same monthly data allowance on their mobile phone contract.

   Dave has used $\frac{4}{7}$ of his monthly data allowance.

   Elaine has used $\frac{5}{8}$ of her monthly data allowance.

   Who has used the most data?

   Give a reason for your answer.

   2

2. Alzena drove from Glasgow to Manchester Airport, 252 miles away.

   Alzena left Glasgow at 11.25 pm.

   She arrived at Manchester Airport at 3.25 am.

   (a) How long did Alzena's journey take ?

   1

   (b) Calculate her average speed in miles per hour for the journey.

   2

   Total marks 3

MARKS | DO NOT WRITE IN THIS MARGIN

3. A charity had a stall at a fair selling crafts and cakes to raise money.

   The stall had sales worth £70.

   The charity must pay 15% of the money from the sales to the organisers.

   The materials for the crafts and cakes cost £24.

   What is the **net** amount of money raised?   2

MARKS | DO NOT WRITE IN THIS MARGIN

4. Three friends decide to tidy up their garden.

The tasks which need to be done are shown in the table below:

Tasks	Detail	Preceding task	Time (minutes)
A	Clear rubbish from the garden	None	10
B	Get lawnmower and edge shears out of the shed	None	5
C	Get hedge trimmer out of the shed	None	5
D	Cut grass in the garden	A, B	30
E	Trim edges of the lawn with shears	B, D	10
F	Cut the hedge	C	20
G	Put grass clippings in bag	D, E	5
H	Put hedge clippings in bag	F	5
I	Take bags to recycling centre	G, H	45

(a) Complete the chart below by writing the letter of the tasks and time (in minutes) in the boxes.   **2**

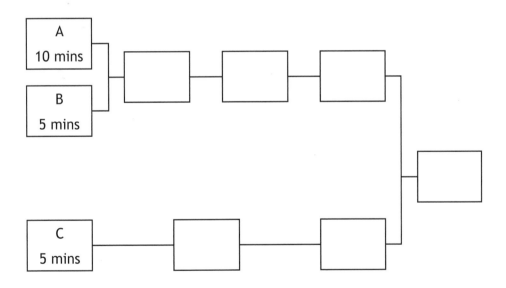

(b) Calculate how much time **in total** the three friends should allow for the garden to be completed?   **1**

Total marks   **3**

MARKS | DO NOT WRITE IN THIS MARGIN

5. Callum, a fitness instructor, is working with ten adults.

He records their resting pulse rates in beats per minute (bpm).

He then takes them on a "Step" exercise session and records their pulse rates immediately after this exercise.

Callum allows the adults to return to their resting pulse rates.

He then takes them on a "Rowing" exercise session and records their pulse rates immediately after this exercise.

The results are displayed in the table below:

Adult		A	B	C	D	E	F	G	H	I	J
Resting pulse rate (bpm)		60	70	64	78	58	93	62	72	82	90
After Step pulse rate (bpm)		105	115	109	120	102	120	112	118	124	130
After Rowing pulse rate (bpm)		102	117	100	110	100	120	105	107	112	120

MARKS

Question 5 (continued)

Callum has drawn the following scattergraph of the pulse rate results for the **step** exercise, and marked in a line of best fit.

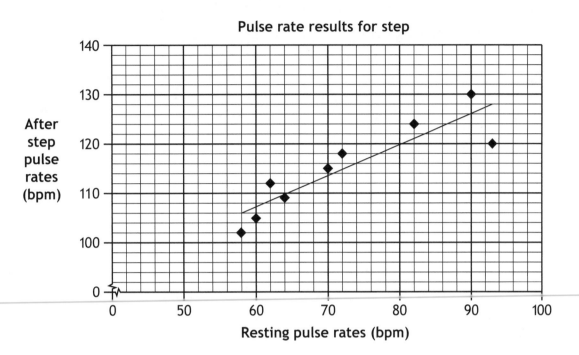

(a) Mark in the pulse rate results for **rowing** on the grid below.   2

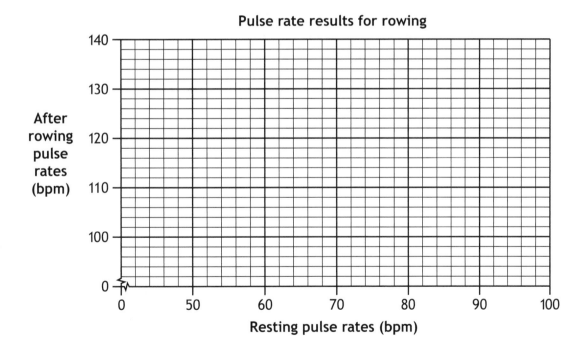

(b) Draw a line of best fit on the diagram above.   1

MARKS | DO NOT WRITE IN THIS MARGIN

Question 5 (continued)

(c) A new member of the group had a resting pulse rate of 87. After exercise his pulse rate was 112.

Which exercise do you think he is likely to have done?

Give a reason for your answer. **2**

Total marks 5

MARKS | DO NOT WRITE IN THIS MARGIN

6. The table below shows the average monthly exchange rates for British pounds (GBP) to euros (EUR) between January and July 2012.

Foreign Exchange Conversion Data
1 GBP to Euros

Jan Feb Mar Apr May Jun Jul Aug Sep Oct Nov Dec

Average Monthly Rates

January	1·2018 EUR
February	1·1949 EUR
March	1·1984 EUR
April	1·2166 EUR
May	1·2435 EUR
June	1·2410 EUR
July	1·2637 EUR

Using the information above, how many more euros would I have received if I changed £500 when the exchange rate was at its highest in comparison to its lowest?

Show all your working.

4

MARKS | DO NOT WRITE IN THIS MARGIN

7. In a **square** plain glass panel, a designer wants to place a coloured triangular piece of glass as shown in the diagram below.

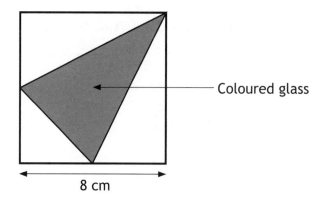

Coloured glass

8 cm

The triangular piece of coloured glass is formed from a corner of the square to the mid points of the opposite edges as shown in the diagram.

Calculate the ratio of the area of **coloured** glass to the area of **plain** glass.   4

Show all your working.

MARKS

8. Jill earns £24 300 per annum.

   She has a personal tax allowance of £8130.

   She pays tax at the basic rate of 20%.

   (a) Calculate how much tax she must pay each year.   **2**

   (b) Jill also pays £166·08 **per month** in National Insurance and £100 **per month** into her pension.

       (i) Calculate Jill's **total monthly** deductions.   **2**

       (ii) Calculate Jill's **monthly** take home pay.   **1**

                       Total marks   **5**

9. The 'Accessibility Guidelines for Buildings and Facilities for Wheelchair Access' give two recommendations.

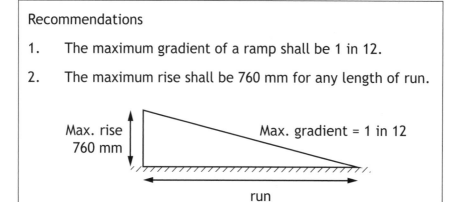

Recommendations

1.　The maximum gradient of a ramp shall be 1 in 12.

2.　The maximum rise shall be 760 mm for any length of run.

Max. rise 760 mm

Max. gradient = 1 in 12

run

The drawing below shows the design of a **new ramp**.

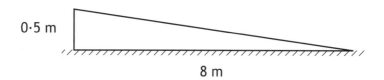

0·5 m

8 m

(a)　Does the new ramp meet Recommendation 1 ?

　　Give a reason.　　　　　　2

(b)　Does the new ramp meet Recommendation 2 ?

　　Give a reason.　　　　　　1

Total marks　3

10. Juma recorded his golf scores over the year. He played 12 times in windy conditions and 12 times in calm conditions.

The data for the windy conditions are illustrated in the box plot below.

Windy conditions

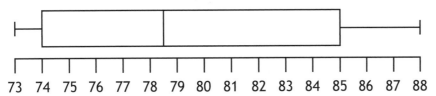

73 74 75 76 77 78 79 80 81 82 83 84 85 86 87 88

His scores for the calm conditions are shown in the table below.

Calm conditions

70	68	73	70
67	78	74	73
74	76	78	76

(a) Construct a box plot to illustrate the data for Juma's golf scores in calm conditions.

3

MARKS | DO NOT WRITE IN THIS MARGIN

Question 10 (continued)

(b) State a valid comparison between the scores for the windy and calm conditions.

1

Total marks   **4**

[END OF SPECIMEN QUESTION PAPER]

MARKS

ADDITIONAL SPACE FOR ANSWERS

MARKS DO NOT WRITE IN THIS MARGIN

ADDITIONAL SPACE FOR ANSWERS

MARKS

N5

National Qualifications
SPECIMEN ONLY

Mark

SQ26/N5/02

Lifeskills Mathematics
Paper 2

Date — Not applicable

Duration — 1 hour and 40 minutes

Fill in these boxes and read what is printed below.

Full name of centre

Town

Forename(s)

Surname

Number of seat

Date of birth

Day	Month	Year
D D	M M	Y Y

Scottish candidate number

Total marks — 55

You may use a calculator.

Attempt ALL questions.

Use **blue** or **black** ink. Pencil may be used for graphs and diagrams only.

Write your working and answers in the spaces provided. Additional space for answers is provided at the end of this booklet. If you use this space, write clearly the number of the question you are attempting.

Square-ruled paper is provided at the back of this booklet.

Full credit will be given only to solutions which contain appropriate working.

State the units for your answer where appropriate.

Before leaving the examination room you must give this booklet to the Invigilator.
If you do not, you may lose all the marks for this paper.

FORMULAE LIST

Circumference of a circle: $C = \pi d$

Area of a circle: $A = \pi r^2$

Theorem of Pythagoras:

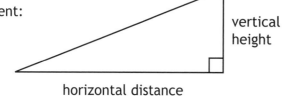

$a^2 + b^2 = c^2$

Volume of a cylinder: $V = \pi r^2 h$

Volume of a prism: $V = Ah$

Standard deviation: $s = \sqrt{\dfrac{\Sigma(x - \bar{x})^2}{n-1}} = \sqrt{\dfrac{\Sigma x^2 - (\Sigma x)^2/n}{n-1}}$, where n is the sample size.

Gradient:

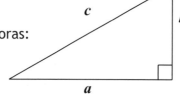

vertical height

horizontal distance

$$\text{gradient} = \frac{\text{vertical height}}{\text{horizontal distance}}$$

MARKS | DO NOT WRITE IN THIS MARGIN

Attempt ALL questions

1. A triathlon is a competition involving swimming, cycling and running.

   It has 3 stages. Competitors aim to complete each stage within the target time.

   The table below shows information about different triathlon events.

Name of triathlon event	Stage 1	Stage 2	Stage 3
Super Sprint	Swim 400 m Target time: 8 mins	Cycle 10 km Target time: 18 mins	Run 2·5 km Target time: 10 mins
Sprint	Swim 750 m Target time: 11 mins	Cycle 20 km Target time: 30 mins	Run 5 km Target time: 17 mins
Olympic	Swim 1500 m Target time: 23 mins	Cycle 40 km Target time: 60 mins	Run 10 km Target time: 35 mins

(a) What is the total distance (in kilometres) for the **Sprint** event?   1

(b) If the **Olympic** swim is completed **exactly** on the target time, what would be the average speed in metres per minute?   2

MARKS

DO NOT WRITE IN THIS MARGIN

Question 1 (continued)

(c) If Joe completed Stage 2 of the **Super Sprint** event at an average speed of 25 kilometres per hour, was he within the target time?

Give a reason for your answer.   **2**

Total marks   5

MARKS | DO NOT WRITE IN THIS MARGIN

2. To use a Fun Park you can either buy:

   • unlimited ride wristbands or
   • a Fun Park Pass and single tokens.

   The prices are given below.

Price list	
Individual unlimited ride wristband	£35·00
Family of four unlimited ride wristband	£91·00
Fun Park Pass per person	£5·00
Single tokens (each)	£1·00

Ride	Number of tokens required
Ghost Train	3
Dodgems	3
Zero Gravity	6
Flying Rockets	3
White Water Ride	3
Big Splash Mountain	3

The Oliver family consists of 2 adults and 2 children.

(a) Calculate how much it would cost the Oliver family to buy Fun Park Passes and enough single tokens for each of them to go once on the Ghost Train, Dodgems and Zero Gravity.

2

MARKS | DO NOT WRITE IN THIS MARGIN

Question 2 (continued)

(b) The Oliver family thinks that buying Fun Park passes and single tokens is the cheapest way to go on these 3 rides.

Is the Oliver family correct? Use your working to justify your answer.   **2**

(c) The Oliver family wants to return next week to go on **ALL** of the rides once. What will be the cheapest way for them to do this? Show your working.   **4**

Total marks   8

MARKS DO NOT WRITE IN THIS MARGIN

3.

Maxisport/Shutterstock.com

An athlete **without a coach** records the following times (in seconds) in a series of 400 metre races.

47·8   48·3   50·2   49·5   46·9   49·5

The same athlete then decides to train with an athletics coach.

After training with the coach, the athlete runs a series of races which produces a mean of 49·3 seconds and a standard deviation of 0·23.

(a) For the athlete's times **without a coach**, calculate:

    (i)   the mean;   1

    (ii) the standard deviation.   3

(b) Make **two** valid comparisons about the performance of the athlete before and after training with the coach.   2

MARKS

Question 3 (continued)

(c) In the final of the 400 metres sprint at the athletics championship, the following times were recorded, in seconds.

   47·8   47·9   54·8   48·1   48·3   47·1

Calculate:

   (i) the mean;   1

   (ii) the median.   1

(d) Which of the two averages — the mean or the median — is more representative of the data?

Give a reason for your answer.   1

Total marks   9

MARKS | DO NOT WRITE IN THIS MARGIN

4. Orla and Mark want a new kitchen.

They investigate various options to borrow the money they need and to pay it back **in one year**. The following information is what they found out.

The best rates for fixed amounts are from EasyBank as shown in the table below.

Loan Amount	£2500		£5000		£10 000	
Interest per year	17%		14·6%		12·26%	
Repayment terms over 1 year	Monthly	Total	Monthly	Total	Monthly	Total
	£243·75	A	£477·50	£5730	B	£11 226

(a) What is the total repayment **(A)** on a loan of £2500 from EasyBank?   1

(b) What is the monthly repayment **(B)** on a loan of £10 000 from EasyBank?   1

(c) Calculate the difference in total repayments between Orla and Mark taking out a loan of £5000 each, compared with a single loan of £10 000 from EasyBank.   2

(d) Orla and Mark also consider using a home improvement loan from a finance company to buy a kitchen. The finance company charges 27·5% simple interest on the loan amount. Calculate the total amount to be repaid for a loan of £5000.   2

MARKS

DO NOT WRITE IN THIS MARGIN

Question 4 (continued)

(e) Calculate the difference between the total amount to be repaid on a £5000 loan from EasyBank, compared with the total amount to be repaid using the home improvement loan.   1

(f) Orla and Mark also consider using a store card to buy a kitchen. The kitchen costs £5000. The store card offers a 10% discount on the price of the kitchen. It then charges simple interest of 19·9% on the balance.

Compare the option of using the store card with the option of taking out a loan of £5000 from EasyBank for a year.

Would the store card be a good option? Use your calculations to justify your answer.   4

Total marks 11

MARKS | DO NOT WRITE IN THIS MARGIN

5. For an end-of-term party, the teacher brought in a 2 litre bottle of **undiluted** orange juice.

The 2 litre bottle of undiluted orange juice has to be mixed with 4 times the amount of water.

The teacher **diluted** the orange juice and then poured it into cylindrical glasses with a radius of 4 cm and a height of 10 cm.

(a) If a space of 1 cm is left at the top of each glass, how many pupils will be able to get a glass of orange juice?   **5**

(b) If all of the diluted orange juice is poured into 25 of these cylindrical glasses so that each contains the same amount, what depth of orange juice will be in glass?

Write your answer to the nearest centimetre.   **4**

Total marks   **9**

MARKS | DO NOT WRITE IN THIS MARGIN

6. Isaac lives in Edinburgh. He is planning a trip to Europe.

He has saved £1800 for his expenses, travel and accommodation.

He intends to:

- stay 1 night in London on his way to Europe, 12 nights in Berlin, 10 nights in Zurich and 1 night in London on the way home;

- travel by train;

- budget £30 per night for expenses in London, £38 per night in Berlin and £45 per night in Zurich.

He gets the following information from the internet.

London accommodation	Price per night
James Square Hostel	£9
St Ethins Hotel	£49
City Sights Hotel	£41

Berlin accommodation	Price per night
Budget Hostel	€53
One45° Hostel	€13
Astel Haus Hostel	€15

Zurich accommodation	Price per night
Zurich Hostel	CHF 51
Swiss Youth Hostel	CHF 118
Hotel Hattingon	CHF 125
Martha Bed and Breakfast	CHF 113

Question 6 (continued)

TRAIN TIMES and PRICES		
Route	Departure/Arrival Times	Price (GBP) one way
Edinburgh — London	dep 0800 — arr 1246	60·50
	dep 0830 — arr 1254	73·50
London — Berlin	dep 0835 — arr 2125	112·00
	dep 1504 — arr 0112	39·00
Berlin — Zurich	dep 0948 — arr 1128	56·00
	dep 1141 — arr 1800	103·00
Zurich — London	dep 0934 — arr 1639	188·50
London — Edinburgh	dep 0930 — arr 1415	69·00
	dep 1000 — arr 1524	87·00

FOREIGN EXCHANGE RATES	
POUNDS STERLING (£)	OTHER CURRENCIES
1	€1·28 (Euros)
1	CHF 1·53 (Swiss Francs)

(a) Isaac decides to choose the **cheapest** accommodation for his trip. Calculate the **total** cost of his accommodation. Use the foreign exchange information above to give your answer in pounds sterling.

6

MARKS

Question 6 (continued)

(b) Isaac also chooses the **cheapest** train journey for each stage of his trip. Find the **total** cost of the train journeys.

2

(c) Does Isaac have enough money, within his £1800 budget, to pay for his chosen accommodation, train journeys and expenses?   Use your calculations to justify your answer.

5

Total marks 13

[END OF SPECIMEN QUESTION PAPER]

ADDITIONAL SPACE FOR ANSWERS

ADDITIONAL SPACE FOR ANSWERS

Page sixteen

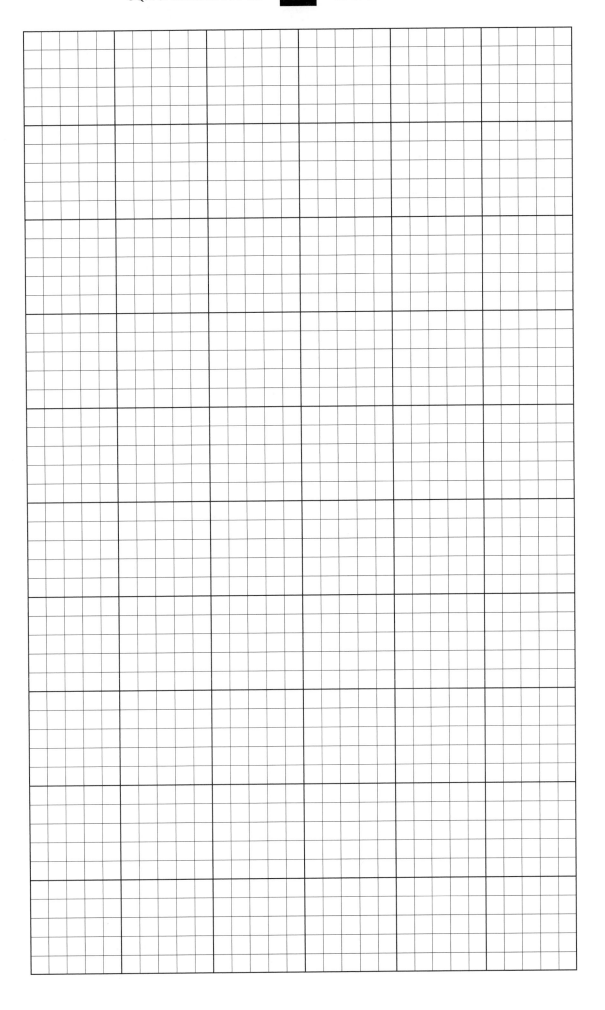

Model Paper 1

Whilst this Model Practice Paper has been specially commissioned by Hodder Gibson for use as practice for the National 5 exams, the key reference documents remain the SQA Specimen Paper 2013 and the SQA Past Paper 2014.

National
Qualifications
MODEL PAPER 1

Lifeskills Mathematics
Paper 1
(Non-Calculator)

Duration — 50 minutes

Total marks — 35

You may NOT use a calculator.

Attempt ALL questions.

Use **blue** or **black** ink. Pencil may be used for graphs and diagrams only.

Write your working and answers in the spaces provided. Additional space for answers is provided at the end of this booklet. If you use this space, write clearly the number of the question you are attempting.

Square-ruled paper is provided at the back of this booklet.

Full credit will be given only to solutions which contain appropriate working.

State the units for your answer where appropriate.

Before leaving the examination room you must give this booklet to the Invigilator.
If you do not, you may lose all the marks for this paper.

HODDER
GIBSON
LEARN MORE

FORMULAE LIST

Circumference of a circle: $C = \pi d$

Area of a circle: $A = \pi r^2$

Theorem of Pythagoras:

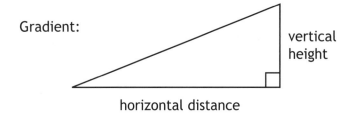

$a^2 + b^2 = c^2$

Volume of a cylinder: $V = \pi r^2 h$

Volume of a prism: $V = Ah$

Standard deviation: $s = \sqrt{\dfrac{\Sigma(x - \bar{x})^2}{n - 1}} = \sqrt{\dfrac{\Sigma x^2 - (\Sigma x)^2/n}{n - 1}}$, where n is the sample size.

Gradient:

vertical height

horizontal distance

$\text{gradient} = \dfrac{\text{vertical height}}{\text{horizontal distance}}$

MARKS DO NOT WRITE IN THIS MARGIN

Attempt ALL questions

1. Dawn asked her friends how many emails they sent in a day.

   The results are shown below.

   13   21   25   32   16   18   25   23   5   17   9   30

   Find the median number of emails sent.   **2**

2. A kilometre is about $\frac{5}{8}$ of a mile.

   How many kilometres would be equivalent to 28 miles?   **2**

MARKS | DO NOT WRITE IN THIS MARGIN

3. Stacii and Ellis are playing a game using two spinners, as shown.

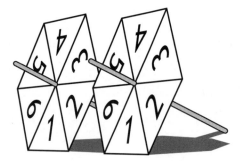

Stacii needs the spinners to land on two threes **or** two fours to win the game.

What is the probability that she will win the game?   2

4. Patricia's income is £400 per month.

Her outgoings are £370 per month.

Patricia wants to save up for an iPad mini costing £370.

(a) How much money does she have each month after her outgoings are paid?   1

(b) If she can put all this towards the iPad, how many months will it be before she can pay for the iPad?   2

Total marks   3

MARKS | DO NOT WRITE IN THIS MARGIN

5. Hope wants to send four small packets, by ship, to the USA.

The total weight of the four packets is 4 kilograms.

She checks out the adverts for two shipping companies.

	ShipEasy	Ships RU	
		Small	Large
Total weight of packets	0 to 5kg	<2kg	>2kg
Charge per packet	£2.50	£0	£3
Charge per ½ kg	£1.80	£2.10	£1.50

With which company should Hope send her packets?   3

6. A gardener collected data on two types of tomato.

The box plots below shows data for the masses, in grams, of the tomatoes in the two samples.

Make two statements comparing the two types and advise the gardener which type of tomato he should grow in future.

3

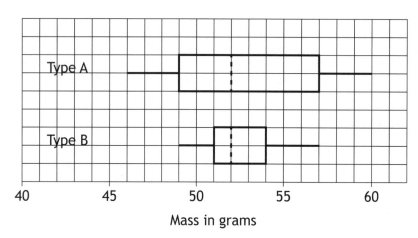

Mass in grams

MARKS

7. Akib intends to drive from Edinburgh to Southampton, a distance of 420 miles, for a meeting.

   He intends to drive overnight, to avoid traffic.

   He needs to be in Southampton for 0730 on Monday morning.

   He expects to be able to average 50 miles per hour.

   He will have a stop for coffee of 30 minutes, and a stop to re-fuel of 20 minutes.

   At what time, **to the nearest quarter of an hour**, should Akib leave Edinburgh?   **4**

8. Mr Smith does a survey with 12 students in his maths class.

He asks them how many hours in the week prior to a test they spent revising.

He also recorded the score they achieved for the test.

The results are shown in the table below.

Student	A	B	C	D	E	F	G	H	I	J	K	L
Hours spent revising	2	3	6	4	2	5	4	8	1	7	9	2
Score in test %	60	70	80	65	50	60	50	80	30	60	80	50

(a) Plot this data, as a scattergraph, on the grid below.   2

(b) Draw a line of best fit.   2

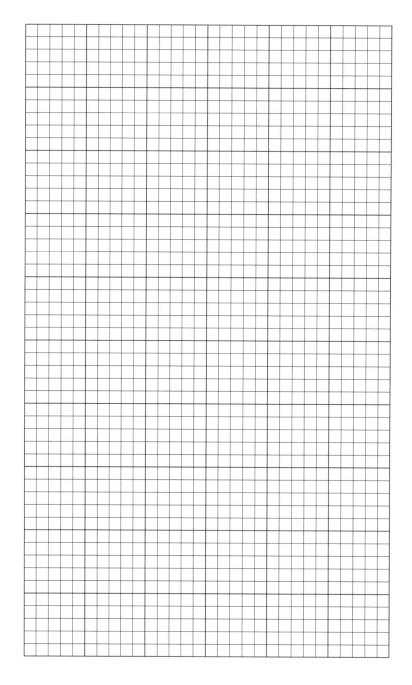

Question 8 (continued)

(c) Student "I" would like to improve his grade to 60%.   **2**

How many **extra** hours should he revise in the week before his test, if he is to achieve this?

Total marks   6

MARKS DO NOT WRITE IN THIS MARGIN

9. Camray is 25 miles due north of Dunray.

Earay lies to the east side of the road joining Camray to Dunray, and is 47 miles from Camray and 63 miles from Dunray. (All roads are straight.)

(a) Make a scale drawing of the above, using a scale of 1mm = 1 mile.   4

(b) What is the three figure bearing of Earay from Camray?   2

Total marks   6

MARKS | DO NOT WRITE IN THIS MARGIN

10. A manufacturer needs to order bolts of 35mm. A tolerance of ±2mm is acceptable.

The manufacturer requires an accuracy rate of better than 80%.

Two companies send a sample of bolts as set out below.

Bolts'R'Us	35mm	33mm	38mm	36mm	37mm	32mm	35mm	34mm
U Bolt	34mm	35mm	34mm	37mm	32mm	33mm	35mm	35mm

From which of the two companies above should the manufacturer order?

Justify your answer.   4

[END OF MODEL PRACTICE PAPER]

ADDITIONAL SPACE FOR ANSWERS

MARKS

ADDITIONAL SPACE FOR ANSWERS

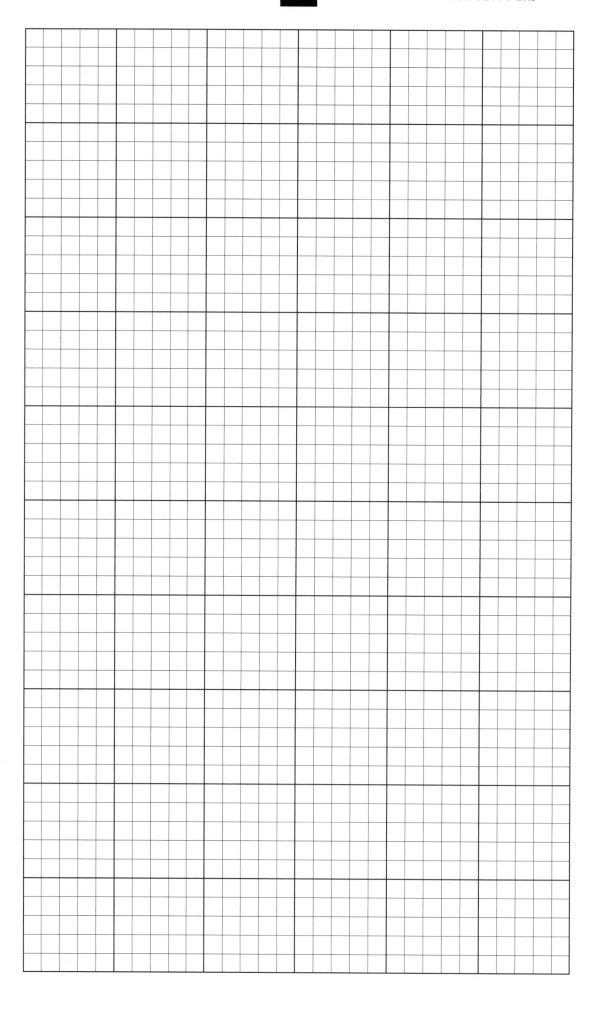

National Qualifications
MODEL PAPER 1

Lifeskills Mathematics
Paper 2

Duration — 1 hour and 40 minutes

Total marks — 55

You may use a calculator.

Attempt ALL questions.

Use **blue** or **black** ink. Pencil may be used for graphs and diagrams only.

Write your working and answers in the spaces provided. Additional space for answers is provided at the end of this booklet. If you use this space, write clearly the number of the question you are attempting.

Square-ruled paper is provided at the back of this booklet.

Full credit will be given only to solutions which contain appropriate working.

State the units for your answer where appropriate.

Before leaving the examination room you must give this booklet to the Invigilator.
If you do not, you may lose all the marks for this paper.

HODDER
GIBSON
LEARN MORE

FORMULAE LIST

Circumference of a circle: $C = \pi d$

Area of a circle: $A = \pi r^2$

Theorem of Pythagoras:

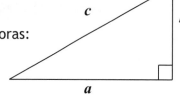

$$a^2 + b^2 = c^2$$

Volume of a cylinder: $V = \pi r^2 h$

Volume of a prism: $V = Ah$

Standard deviation: $s = \sqrt{\dfrac{\Sigma(x - \bar{x})^2}{n-1}} = \sqrt{\dfrac{\Sigma x^2 - (\Sigma x)^2/n}{n-1}}$, where n is the sample size.

Gradient:

vertical height

horizontal distance

$$\text{gradient} = \frac{\text{vertical height}}{\text{horizontal distance}}$$

MARKS | DO NOT WRITE IN THIS MARGIN

Attempt ALL questions

1. Jeremy asked his friends how many text messages they sent in a day.

   The data is shown below.

   11 45 30 10 28 33 17 12 21 19
   35 24 17 52 16 37 23 29 41 30

   Kirsten asked the same question of her friends.

   She constructed a stem and leaf diagram to illustrate her data, as shown below.

1	1 3 5
2	1 2 4 6 6 8 9
3	2 5 5 6 7 7
4	0 3 8
5	4

   Key: n=20

        2|1 represents 21 texts

   (a) Illustrate Jeremy's data on a box plot.   3

MARKS | DO NOT WRITE IN THIS MARGIN

Question 1 (continued)

(b) Does Jeremy or Kirsten have the higher median? **1**

(c) 25% of Kirsten's friends sent fewer than 23 texts.

Is this more or less than the lowest 25% of Jeremy's friends?

Use your working to justify your answer. **1**

Total marks   5

MARKS

2. In January, Tony weighed himself. The scales read 95 kg.

He is going on holiday on the 6th July.

He wants to hit a target weight of 73 kg by then.

On the 1st of February, he hired Calum as his personal trainer. Calum reckoned his programme of exercise and diet would see Tony reduce his weight by 6% each month.

If Calum's programme is successful, will Tony reach his target weight before the date of his holiday?

Use your working to justify your answer.   5

MARKS DO NOT WRITE IN THIS MARGIN

3. Sharon and her assistant Tanya are furniture makers. They are going to make a wooden-framed settee, with cloth-covered foam cushions. The tasks which have to be done by Sharon and Tanya are in the table below.

	Task	Time (days)
A	make wooden arms and legs	3
B	make wooden back	1
C	make wooden base	2
D	cut foam for back and base	1
E	make covers	2
F	fit covers	1
G	put everything together	1

Each task must be done by one person, but some tasks can be done at the same time.

This list gives the order in which the jobs must be done.

B	must be after	C		
A	must be after	B	and	C
D	must be after	B	and	C
E	must be after	D		
F	must be after	E		
G	must be after	All		

The cost of materials is £350.

The cost of "labour" is £65 per day spent making the settee.

MARKS | DO NOT WRITE IN THIS MARGIN

Question 3 (continued)

(a) Construct an appropriate precedence table, and hence an activity network to illustrate this information.   **4**

(b) Calculate the minimum number of days required to make the settee.   **1**

(c) Sharon and Tanya wish to sell the settee to a shop and make a "mark up" of 40%.

What price should they sell the settee for to make this mark up?   **3**

Total marks   **8**

MARKS

4.   Maya is making a kite using bamboo rods and plastic sheeting.

She makes a sketch of the kite, as shown below.

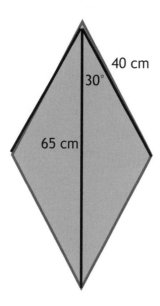

40 cm

30°

65 cm

(a)   Using an appropriate scale make a scale drawing of Maya's kite.

4

MARKS | DO NOT WRITE IN THIS MARGIN

Question 4 (continued)

(b) Use your scale drawing to calculate the total length of bamboo required for the frame, that is, the four sides and the main diagonal.   **2**

(c) Calculate the area of plastic sheeting required to make the kite.   **3**

(d) If Maya decided to strengthen the kite by putting in the other diagonal, what length of bamboo would she require?   **1**

Total marks 10

5. Colin makes dome-shaped clocks as shown.

The dimensions are marked on the diagram.

For transporting to shops, he packs them in cuboid boxes.

The boxes allow 1cm each side of the clock and 1cm on top for packing with polystyrene chips.

These chips cost £50 per cubic metre and the cost of cardboard for packaging is £6.50 per square metre.

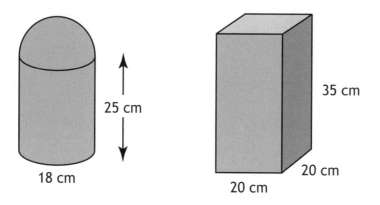

25 cm

18 cm

35 cm

20 cm

20 cm

(a) Calculate the volume occupied by the clock.

4

(b) Calculate the volume required to be filled by chips.

Give your answer to 2 significant figures.

3

MARKS | DO NOT WRITE IN THIS MARGIN

Question 5 (continued)

(c) Calculate, to the nearest penny, the cost of polystyrene chips to pack each box.

2

(d) If Colin only pays for the amount of cardboard used to make the box, what would this cost be?

3

Total marks 12

6. You are the Business Manager in a hospital.

Two drug treatments are recommended to you: Treatment A and Treatment B.

Doctors wish to give the best treatment, but you only have a limited budget.

Your budget is **£3,000,000** per year.

The data on the two treatments are:

Treatment	Survival rate % surviving for 1 year	cost per patient per year £000s
A	61	10.3
B	83	34.1

Assume you have **100 patients** per year.

If you could, you would give all patients Treatment B as it has a better success rate.

But ...

If you treat	100 patients
You would expect	83 to survive
It would cost	100 x £34100 = £3,410,000 so you are over budget.

Remember those who did not survive still received the treatment.

As Business Manager you need to find out the highest number of patients who could be treated with B without going over budget.

Complete this table for 100 patients, calculating the total number expected to survive and the cost of treatment for the different ways of allocating treatments.

No. of patients	No. of survivors	Cost for 1 year	No. of patients	No. of survivors	Cost for 1 year	Total No. survivors	Total cost £millions
Treatment B	1 year	£m	Treatment A	1 year	£m		
100	83	3.41	0	0	0	83	£3.41
75			25				
50			50				
25			75				
0	0	0	100	61	1.03	61	£1.03

9

MARKS | DO NOT WRITE IN THIS MARGIN

Question 6 (continued)

(a) What estimate does this give you for the number of patients who could be treated with B if the hospital is to stay within budget?   1

(b) Complete this graph of total survivors against total cost.   3

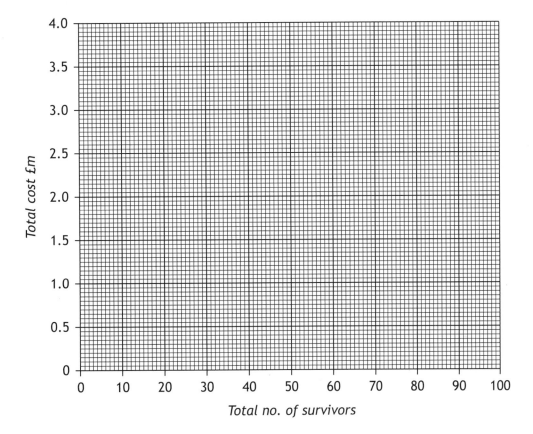

(c) Does this change your estimate?

If so, how many patients would you recommend be treated with B?   2

Total marks 15

[END OF MODEL PRACTICE PAPER]

ADDITIONAL SPACE FOR ANSWERS

ADDITIONAL SPACE FOR ANSWERS

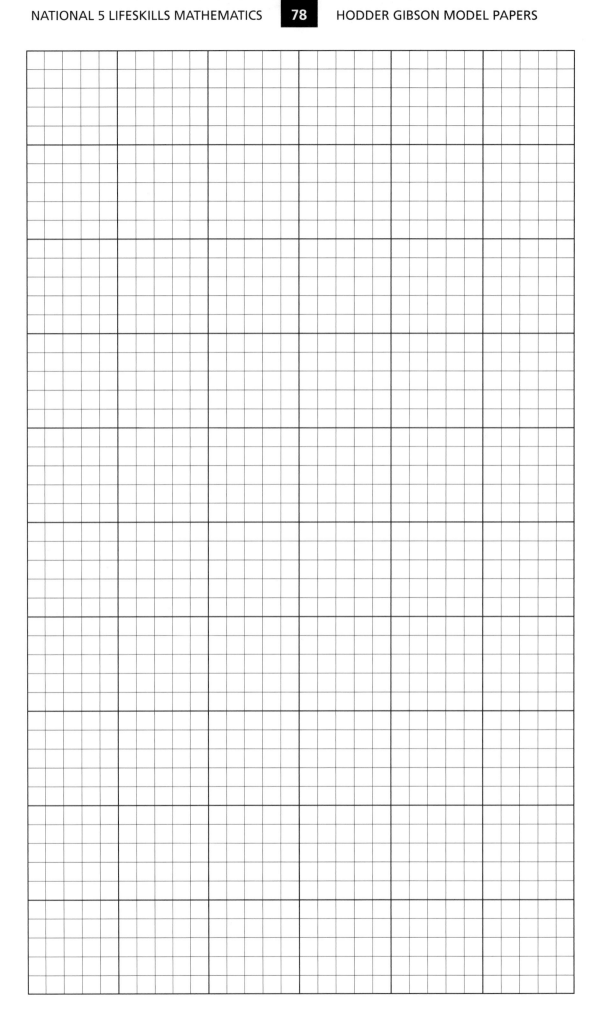

NATIONAL 5

Model Paper 2

Whilst this Model Practice Paper has been specially commissioned by Hodder Gibson for use as practice for the National 5 exams, the key reference documents remain the SQA Specimen Paper 2013 and the SQA Past Paper 2014.

National
Qualifications
MODEL PAPER 2

Lifeskills Mathematics
Paper 1
(Non-Calculator)

Duration — 50 minutes

Total marks — 35

You may NOT use a calculator.

Attempt ALL questions.

Use **blue** or **black** ink. Pencil may be used for graphs and diagrams only.

Write your working and answers in the spaces provided. Additional space for answers is provided at the end of this booklet. If you use this space, write clearly the number of the question you are attempting.

Square-ruled paper is provided at the back of this booklet.

Full credit will be given only to solutions which contain appropriate working.

State the units for your answer where appropriate.

Before leaving the examination room you must give this booklet to the Invigilator.
If you do not, you may lose all the marks for this paper.

HODDER
GIBSON
LEARN MORE

FORMULAE LIST

Circumference of a circle: $C = \pi d$

Area of a circle: $A = \pi r^2$

Theorem of Pythagoras:

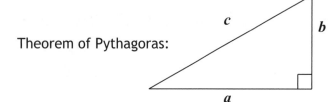

$a^2 + b^2 = c^2$

Volume of a cylinder: $V = \pi r^2 h$

Volume of a prism: $V = Ah$

Standard deviation: $s = \sqrt{\dfrac{\Sigma(x - \bar{x})^2}{n-1}} = \sqrt{\dfrac{\Sigma x^2 - (\Sigma x)^2 / n}{n-1}}$, where n is the sample size.

Gradient:

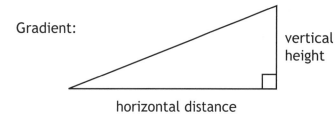

$$\text{gradient} = \frac{\text{vertical height}}{\text{horizontal distance}}$$

MARKS | DO NOT WRITE IN THIS MARGIN

Attempt ALL questions

1. The fuel tank on Sara's car holds 40 litres of fuel.

   The petrol gauge is shown below.

   On a full tank of fuel, the car could travel 560km.

   Sara has 180km left of a journey to complete.

   Will she have enough fuel?

   Use your working to justify your answer.   2

2. Building regulations state that the gradient for an access ramp should be less than 1 in 12.

   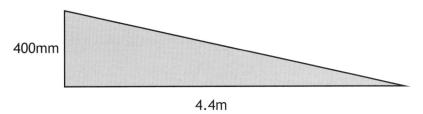

   Does this ramp meet the building regulations?

   Give a reason for your answer.   2

MARKS

3. In a car rally event, Grigor drove the 114km leg in 1½ hours.

    What was his average speed in km per hour?   3

4. Simiran wants a piece of wood for a frame. She needs it to be 15cm ±2mm.

    Between which two measurements would Simiran accept a piece of wood?   2

MARKS

5. In a sponsored swim, a number of students raised money for a local charity.

    The distance each student swam and the money raised is shown in the table.

Name	Distance (metres)	Amount
Mark	300	£12
Kai	500	£20
Caroline	200	£4
Kevin	400	£10
Satveer	300	£8
Allan	250	£15
Jack	300	£20
Zahra	50	£10
Lydia	450	£18

(a) Plot this information on a scattergraph.   2

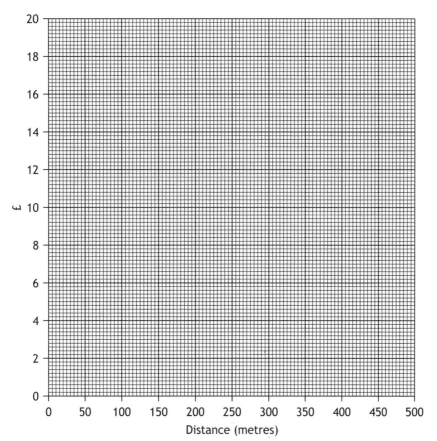

(b) Draw a line of best fit.   2

(c) Alysoun swam 350m. How much would you expect her to raise?   1

Total marks   5

MARKS DO NOT WRITE IN THIS MARGIN

6. Patricia makes artwork from coloured glass.

    If she works for 6 hours in a day, she can make 4 pieces.

    A dealer wants 12 pieces and offers to either:

    •   pay £15 per hour for the time taken to make the pieces, or

    •   pay a fee of £150 plus £9 per piece.

    Which option would earn Patricia more?

    Justify your answer.   5

7. A mast is fixed to the corner of a concrete base as shown in the diagram.

    A wire is fixed from the top of the mast to the opposite corner of the base.

    The base is 4m long and 3m wide.

    The mast is 12m high.

    How long is the wire?   4

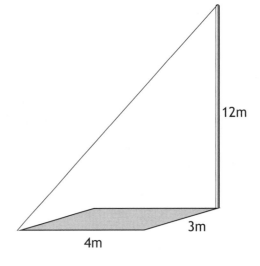

12m

3m

4m

MARKS

8. (a) How many of these tins of soup can be packed into the carton?

2

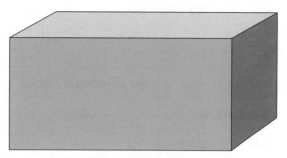

Diameter of tins 7cm,
height 11cm

Carton length 35cm,
width 15cm, height 22cm

(b) If the diameter was reduced to 5 cm and height increased to 13 cm, how many more tins would fit in the box?

2

Total marks   4

9. Michael and his friend Ian are going to redecorate Michael's bedroom, and put in some self-assembly furniture.

They make up a list of tasks and put them in a table to help them to organise the work.

	Task	No of people req'd	Time (hrs)	Preceded by
A	clear room	2	2	—
B	paint woodwork	1	2	A
C	assemble units	1	3	A
D	fit carpet	1	2	A B E
E	hang wallpaper	2	4	A B
F	hang curtains	1	1	A B E
G	tidy up	2	1	A B C D E F

Complete the precedence diagram below, putting the task letter and time in the appropriate box.

How long should Michael and Ian set aside to complete the project?   4

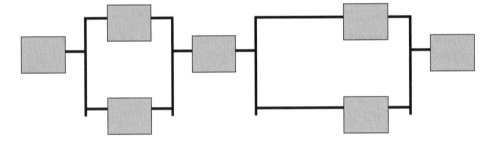

MARKS | DO NOT WRITE IN THIS MARGIN

10. Rory constructed two box plots to show the data he collected on the lifespan of light bulbs produced by two manufacturers.

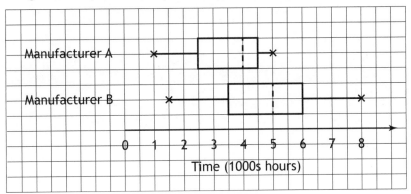

Complete the gaps in this table.

	Manufacturer A	Manufacturer B
Median		5000 hours
Lower Quartile	2500 hours	3500 hours
Upper Quartile	4500 hours	
Range	4000 hours	6500 hours
Interquartile Range	2000 hours	2500 hours

Which manufacturer do you think Rory should choose to supply his light bulbs?   **4**

Justify your answer.

[END OF MODEL PRACTICE PAPER]

ADDITIONAL SPACE FOR ANSWERS

ADDITIONAL SPACE FOR ANSWERS

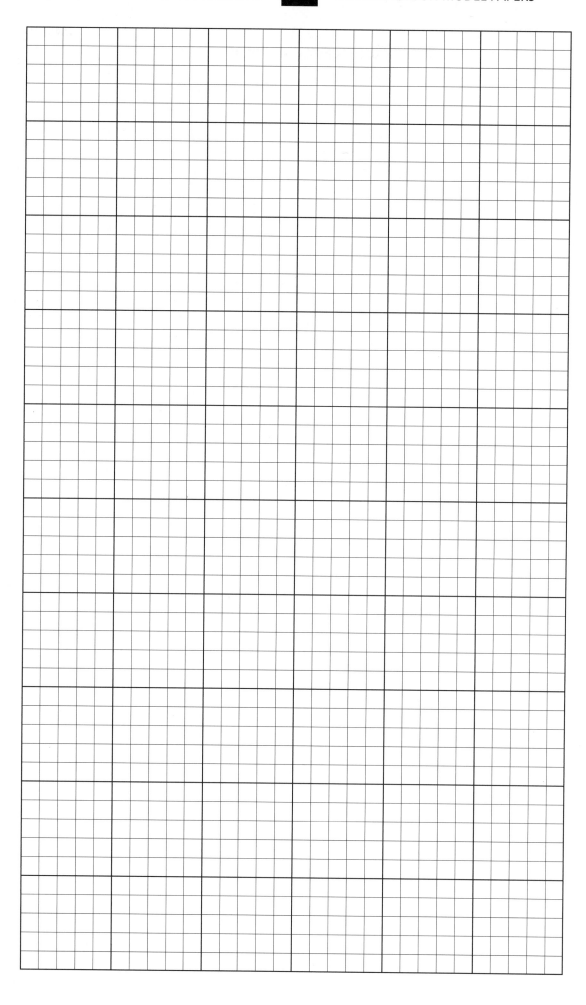

National Qualifications
MODEL PAPER 2

Lifeskills Mathematics
Paper 2

Duration — 1 hour and 40 minutes

Total marks — 55

You may use a calculator.

Attempt ALL questions.

Use **blue** or **black** ink. Pencil may be used for graphs and diagrams only.

Write your working and answers in the spaces provided. Additional space for answers is provided at the end of this booklet. If you use this space, write clearly the number of the question you are attempting.

Square-ruled paper is provided at the back of this booklet.

Full credit will be given only to solutions which contain appropriate working.

State the units for your answer where appropriate.

Before leaving the examination room you must give this booklet to the Invigilator.
If you do not, you may lose all the marks for this paper.

FORMULAE LIST

Circumference of a circle: $C = \pi d$

Area of a circle: $A = \pi r^2$

Theorem of Pythagoras: 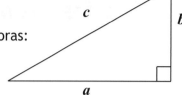 $a^2 + b^2 = c^2$

Volume of a cylinder: $V = \pi r^2 h$

Volume of a prism: $V = Ah$

Standard deviation: $s = \sqrt{\dfrac{\Sigma(x - \bar{x})^2}{n-1}} = \sqrt{\dfrac{\Sigma x^2 - (\Sigma x)^2/n}{n-1}}$, where n is the sample size.

Gradient:

vertical height

horizontal distance

$$\text{gradient} = \frac{\text{vertical height}}{\text{horizontal distance}}$$

Attempt ALL questions

1. Hannah works in a car sales room.

    She earns £16 860 gross in a year.

    Her annual personal allowance is £8105.

    Hannah pays tax at the basic rate of 20%.

    Her contribution towards National Insurance is at a rate of 12% on earnings over £7755.

    Complete the boxes marked A, B, C, D in the payslip below.

    There is a payslip with A, B, C, D removed to allow you to insert values.   **6**

Period	February	Name	H. Belmont		
Pay (£)		Deductions (£)			
Basic	1405	Tax	A	Gross Pay	1405
Overtime	—	N.I.	B	Deduction	C
Total pay	1405	Total deduction	C	Net pay	D

Period	February	Name	H. Belmont		
Pay (£)		Deductions (£)			
Basic	1405	Tax		Gross Pay	1405
Overtime	—	N.I.		Deduction	
Total pay	1405	Total deduction		Net pay	

MARKS

2. The Human Resources Manager in a factory recorded how many of the workers were absent each day over a period of 21 days.

The results are listed below.

19	22	19	22	20	21	17
19	21	16	20	19	18	18
20	21	23	19	18	17	19

If 21 or more workers are absent on a given day, the factory has to close down one of the production lines.

(a) Construct a box plot to illustrate this information.   3

(b) What is the probability that, on a day chosen at random from this sample, the factory has to close one of the production lines?   2

Total marks   5

MARKS | DO NOT WRITE IN THIS MARGIN

3. A pharmaceutical company makes vitamin pills in the shape of spheres.

The spheres have a radius of 0.5 centimetres.

The company are considering changing the shape of the vitamin pill to a cylinder.

The cylinder has the same volume as the sphere.

Its diameter is 1.4 centimetres.

1.4cm

The company will pack the vitamin pills in cuboid boxes with dimensions as shown below.

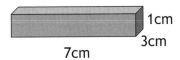

1cm
3cm
7cm

Volume of a sphere $V = 4/3\ \pi r^3$

Volume of a cylinder $V = \pi r^2 h$

(a) What is the volume of the spherical vitamin pill?   3

(b) What is the height of the cylindrical pill?   4

(c) Which shape would allow the company to pack more pills into the box?

Use your working to justify your answer.   3

Total marks 10

MARKS | DO NOT WRITE IN THIS MARGIN

4. Hugh and Kate buy and install a new central heating system in their house.

The system cost £3500.

Once installed, Hugh and Kate record the temperatures over a period of six days.

These temperatures, in degrees Celsius, are shown below.

    19   21   23   21   19   20

Their target temperature for the house is 20° Celsius.

The system is judged to be working efficiently if the mean temperature is within 0.6° of the target temperature and the standard deviation is less than 2° Celsius.

Before installing the system, the monthly cost of heating was £220.

Hugh and Kate think, if the system works efficiently, they can save 15% of this cost.

(a) For the data above, calculate:

    (i) the mean;   **1**

    (ii) the standard deviation.   **3**

(b) Is the system operating effectively?   **2**

    Use your working to justify your answers.

(c) Assuming Hugh and Kate make the savings they think they will make; how many years will it be before the system "pays for itself"?   **3**

Total marks   9

5. Dave and Carol are discussing their health one evening.

Doing some research they discovered the following:

The Body Mass Index (BMI) is a measure used to show if an adult is at a healthy weight.

The formula for calculating BMI is

$$\text{BMI} = \frac{\text{Weight}}{\text{Height}^2} \quad \text{(weight in kilograms)} \quad \text{(height in metres)}$$

		BMI	Category
A person with BMI	between	18.5 and 25	is at a healthy weight.
A person with BMI	less than	18.5	is underweight.
A person with BMI	between	25 and 30	is overweight.
A person with BMI	over	30	is obese.

Most people still work using "Imperial measures".

Dave and Carol note that

1 foot	= 30.5 cm	(or 0.305m)
12 inches	= 1 foot	
1 inch	= 2.54 cm	
1 stone	= 6.35 kg	
14 pounds	= 1 stone	
1 pound	= 0.454 kg	

To stay healthy an average man needs 2500 calories per day.

An average woman needs 2000 calories per day.

Moderate exercise will burn about 8 calories per minute.

Strenuous exercise will burn about 12 calories per minute.

Carol knows she is 1.58 metres tall and weighs 48kg.

Dave knows he is 6 foot tall and weighs 15 stones.

MARKS | DO NOT WRITE IN THIS MARGIN

Question 5 (continued)

(a) Calculate Carol's BMI and state in which category she lies.   3

(b) In which category does Dave lie?   5

(c) Dave calculates that he takes in about 3000 calories in a day.

He decides to go to a gym to try and lose his "excess calories".

Design an exercise programme, lasting about 45 minutes, which mixes strenuous and moderate exercise, and which burns his excess calories.   4

You may wish to use the table to help you.

Possible programme	Strenuous	Moderate	total
Number of minutes			
Number of calories			

Total marks 12

MARKS | DO NOT WRITE IN THIS MARGIN

6. A Search and Rescue helicopter is out on patrol.

The diagram shows the route the helicopter followed.

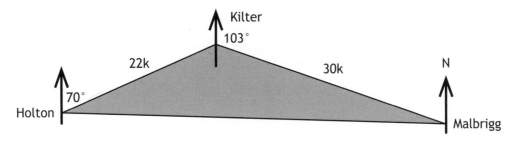

Starting from Holton it flies on a bearing of 070° for 22 kilometres to Kilter.

From Kilter it flies on a bearing of 103° for 30 kilometres to Malbrigg.

The helicopter then flies directly back to Holton.

(a) Using a suitable scale, construct a scale drawing and calculate the total distance travelled by the helicopter. **5**

MARKS

Question 6 (continued)

(b) The helicopter flies at an average speed of 85 kilometres per hour.

It carries enough fuel for 3 hours flying time.

What percentage of fuel will be left when the helicopter returns to Holton?   **4**

(c) A person was reported missing somewhere in the triangle enclosed by the helicopter's trip. Calculate this area.   **4**

[END OF MODEL PRACTICE PAPER]

ADDITIONAL SPACE FOR ANSWERS

ADDITIONAL SPACE FOR ANSWERS

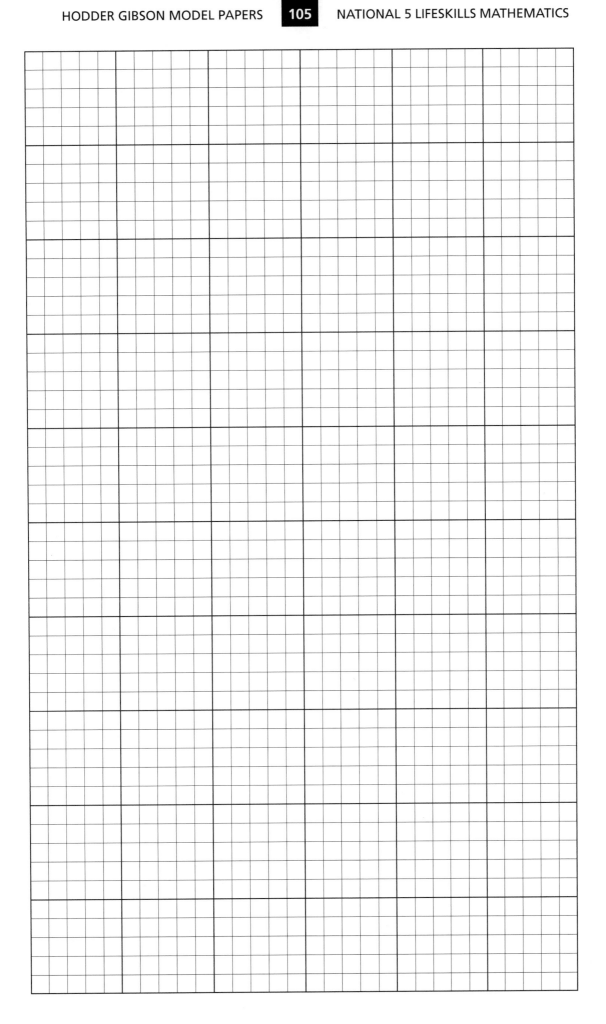

Model Paper 3

Whilst this Model Practice Paper has been specially commissioned by Hodder Gibson for use as practice for the National 5 exams, the key reference documents remain the SQA Specimen Paper 2013 and the SQA Past Paper 2014.

HODDER GIBSON
LEARN MORE

National
Qualifications
MODEL PAPER 3

Lifeskills Mathematics
Paper 1
(Non-Calculator)

Duration — 50 minutes

Total marks — 35

You may NOT use a calculator.

Attempt ALL questions.

Use **blue** or **black** ink. Pencil may be used for graphs and diagrams only.

Write your working and answers in the spaces provided. Additional space for answers is provided at the end of this booklet. If you use this space, write clearly the number of the question you are attempting.

Square-ruled paper is provided at the back of this booklet.

Full credit will be given only to solutions which contain appropriate working.

State the units for your answer where appropriate.

Before leaving the examination room you must give this booklet to the Invigilator.
If you do not, you may lose all the marks for this paper.

HODDER
GIBSON
LEARN MORE

FORMULAE LIST

Circumference of a circle: $C = \pi d$

Area of a circle: $A = \pi r^2$

Theorem of Pythagoras:

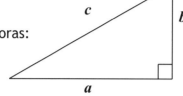

$a^2 + b^2 = c^2$

Volume of a cylinder: $V = \pi r^2 h$

Volume of a prism: $V = Ah$

Standard deviation: $s = \sqrt{\dfrac{\Sigma(x - \bar{x})^2}{n-1}} = \sqrt{\dfrac{\Sigma x^2 - (\Sigma x)^2 / n}{n-1}}$, where n is the sample size.

Gradient:

horizontal distance

vertical height

$\text{gradient} = \dfrac{\text{vertical height}}{\text{horizontal distance}}$

MARKS

Attempt ALL questions

1. On a map ¾ inch represents 60 miles.

   How many miles would be represented by 2 inches? **2**

2. Patrick is paid 15% commission on all sales over £3000.

   What will his commission be if his sales amounted to £6500? **3**

3. Julie writes down her monthly budget to check the "state of her finances"

   This is her spreadsheet:

Income	Expenditure	
£1,525	Mortgage	535
	Council Tax	215
	Food	425
	utilities	185
	Car costs	140

   (a) Does she have a surplus or a deficit? **2**

   Show your working.

   (b) Her car costs increase by 20%. What effect does this have on her budget? **2**

   Total marks **4**

MARKS | DO NOT WRITE IN THIS MARGIN

4. The box plot gives information about the distribution of the weights of bags which were loaded into the hold on a plane.

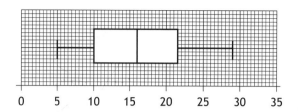

(a) Joseph says the heaviest bag weighs 23kg. Explain why this is not correct.   1

(b) Write down the median weight.   1

(c) Calculate the interquartile range.   1

There are 240 bags on the plane.

(d) Calculate the number of bags with a weight of 10 kg or less.   2

Total marks   5

MARKS | DO NOT WRITE IN THIS MARGIN

5. A surveyor is on site and makes a rough drawing of the triangular plot of land on which some houses are to be built. He marks in the measurements of two sides and angles as shown.

He forgot to mark in the length of the third side.

Make a scale drawing, using a suitable scale, and calculate the length, in metres, of the third side.

4

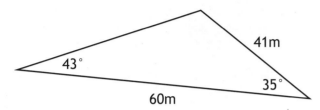

MARKS | DO NOT WRITE IN THIS MARGIN

6. A company wishes to produce a carton which will hold 1 litre of orange juice.

It is looking at two possible cartons, as shown below.

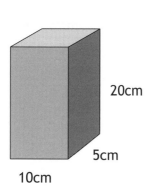
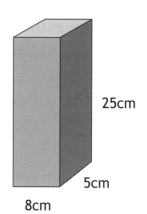

20cm

5cm

10cm

25cm

5cm

8cm

(a) Does each carton hold 1 litre of juice.

Use working to justify your answer.   2

(b) The company will choose the carton which uses least material to make.

Which carton should the company choose?

Justify your answer.   3

Total marks   5

MARKS | DO NOT WRITE IN THIS MARGIN

7. Christine and her brother, Tom, are playing a board game.

The game has two sets of cards as shown:

On her turn, Christine picks a day card and a time card.

(a) Complete this table to show all Christine's possible selections.   1

	9	11	2	5
Mon	M, 9			
Tues	T, 9	T, 11		
Wed	W, 9	W, 11	W, 2	
Thu	Th, 9	Th, 11		
Fri		F, 11	F, 2	F, 5

(b) What is the probability that Christine will pick a Wednesday and a time which is in the afternoon?   2

Total marks   3

MARKS | DO NOT WRITE IN THIS MARGIN

8. A company makes washers with a thickness of 2·3 millimetres to the nearest 0·05 mm.

    (a) Write down the minimum and maximum acceptable thickness of washer.   **1**

    (b) A Quality control Inspector for the company takes samples of each batch made and measures the thicknesses. The results of one sample taken are shown below.

    2·31   2·25   2·19   2·32   2·27   2·29   2·18   2·26   2·30   2·30

    2·36   2·26   2·34   2·35   2·21   2·26   2·26   2·32   2·27   2·27

    If more than 20% are not within tolerance, the machine would have to be re-set.

    Will the machine need to be re-set? Use your working to justify your answer.   **3**

Total marks   **4**

MARKS

9. As part of a class survey, Heather measures the height and foot size of ten of her classmates.

The results are shown in the table below.

Height (cm)	Foot size
152	5
166	6
146	4
138	4
155	6
154	5
176	8
165	6
128	3
178	9

(a) Plot this data in a scatter diagram below. 2

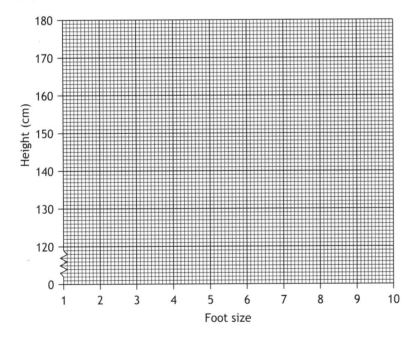

(b) Draw a line of best fit. 2

(c) Gemma, a new pupil, joins the class. She has size 7 feet.

What height would you expect Gemma to be? 1

Total marks 5

[END OF MODEL PRACTICE PAPER]

ADDITIONAL SPACE FOR ANSWERS

Page ten

MARKS

ADDITIONAL SPACE FOR ANSWERS

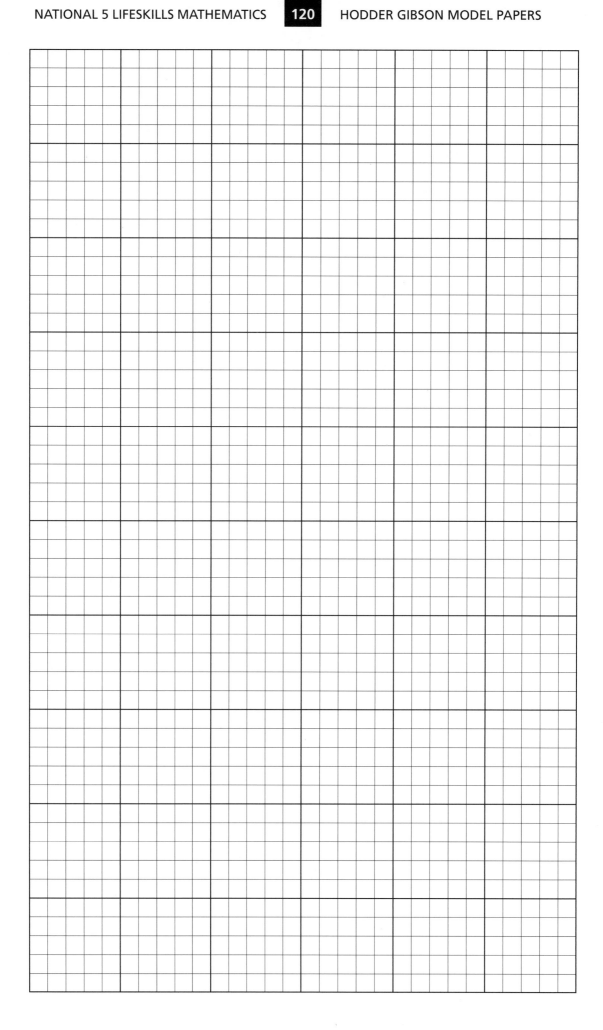

National Qualifications
MODEL PAPER 3

Lifeskills Mathematics
Paper 2

Duration — 1 hour and 40 minutes

Total marks — 55

You may use a calculator.

Attempt ALL questions.

Use **blue** or **black** ink. Pencil may be used for graphs and diagrams only.

Write your working and answers in the spaces provided. Additional space for answers is provided at the end of this booklet. If you use this space, write clearly the number of the question you are attempting.

Square-ruled paper is provided at the back of this booklet.

Full credit will be given only to solutions which contain appropriate working.

State the units for your answer where appropriate.

Before leaving the examination room you must give this booklet to the Invigilator.
If you do not, you may lose all the marks for this paper.

FORMULAE LIST

Circumference of a circle: $C = \pi d$

Area of a circle: $A = \pi r^2$

Theorem of Pythagoras:

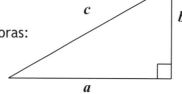

$a^2 + b^2 = c^2$

Volume of a cylinder: $V = \pi r^2 h$

Volume of a prism: $V = Ah$

Standard deviation: $s = \sqrt{\dfrac{\Sigma(x - \bar{x})^2}{n-1}} = \sqrt{\dfrac{\Sigma x^2 - (\Sigma x)^2 / n}{n-1}}$, where n is the sample size.

Gradient:

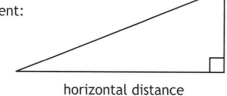

vertical
height

horizontal distance

$$\text{gradient} = \frac{\text{vertical height}}{\text{horizontal distance}}$$

MARKS | DO NOT WRITE IN THIS MARGIN

Attempt ALL questions

1. Melissa works in a bakery as a quality control inspector. One day she takes a sample of six fruit loaves and records the weight, in grams, of each loaf. The weights are as below.

$$395 \quad 400 \quad 408 \quad 390 \quad 405 \quad 402$$

The mean of this data is 400.

(a) Calculate the standard deviation for this data. **3**

(b) New methods are introduced in an attempt to ensure more consistent weights.

Melissa takes another sample and she finds the mean and standard deviation to be 400 grams and 5.8 grams respectively.

Are the new methods successful?

Justify your answer. **2**

Total marks **5**

2. Jim keeps his washing in a basket like the one shown below.

The basket is in the shape of a prism with dimensions as shown.

The height of the basket is 50 centimetres.

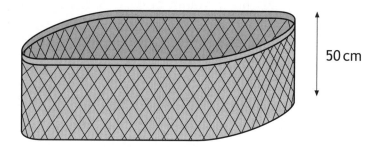

The cross section of the basket consists of a rectangle and two semi-circles, with measurements as shown.

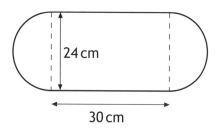

Along with this basket, Jim keeps his ironing in a storage box which has half the volume of the basket.

The storage box is in the shape of a cuboid, 35 centimetres long and 28 centimetres broad.

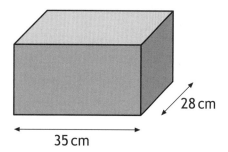

MARKS | DO NOT WRITE IN THIS MARGIN

Question 2 (continued)

(a) Calculate the volume of Jim's washing basket.

Give your answer to three significant figures.   4

(b) Jim has a space, 30 cm high, in a cupboard.

Will his ironing box fit in this space?

Use your working to justify your answer.   4

Total marks   8

3. Phil and Rebecca work in a telesales centre.

The stem and leaf diagram below shows the number of contacts they made over a number of days.

Rebecca		Phil
1	3	
9	4	7 9
8 7 4 3 2 2	5	2 3 4 4 6 6 7 9
9 4	6	3
9 6 3	7	4 8
8 1	8	7
N=15		n=14

Key   1 | 7   represents 71   8 | 7   represents 87

Their boss, Jon, draws a box plot of one of the sets of data.

This is shown below.

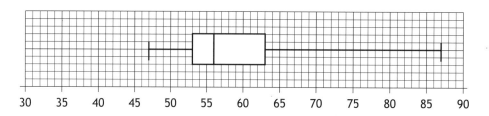

30   35   40   45   50   55   60   65   70   75   80   85   90

(a) Does this box plot represent Phil or Rebecca's data?

     Give a reason for your answer.   1

MARKS | DO NOT WRITE IN THIS MARGIN

Question 3 (continued)

(b) For the other data, find

(i) the median

(ii) the lower quartile

(iii) the upper quartile.   3

(c) Use your answer to construct a box plot for this data.

3

(d) Make a valid statement about the distribution of the data in the two sets.   1

Total marks   8

MARKS | DO NOT WRITE IN THIS MARGIN

4. Alan is a Finance Manager for a company which sells smartboards.

He regularly travels from Edinburgh to London.

The distance from Edinburgh to London is approximately 650 kilometres.

He is looking at a table of carbon dioxide emissions from cars. He knows this is one of the gases which adds to the "Greenhouse Effect" and global warming.

The Government has put cars into thirteen tax bands, based on their carbon dioxide emissions. The table below shows tax band and cost of Road Tax.

* g/km is grams per kilometre

Band	CO_2 emission (g/km*)	12-months rate	6-months rate
A	Up to 100	£0.00	Not available
B	101–110	£20.00	Not available
C	111–120	£30.00	Not available
D	121–130	£105.00	£57.75
E	131–140	£125.00	£68.75
F	141–150	£140.00	£77.00
G	151–165	£175.00	£96.25
H	166–175	£200.00	£110.00
I	176–185	£220.00	£121.00
J	186–200	£260.00	£143.00
K	201–225	£280.00	£154.00
L	226–255	£475.00	£261.25
M	Over 255	£490.00	£269.50

Alan also looks up tables giving CO_2 emissions for other forms of transport.

Transport	Kilograms of CO_2 per passenger per kilometre
Air	0.175
Coach	0.029
Rail	0.061

MARKS | DO NOT WRITE IN THIS MARGIN

Question 4 (continued)

Alan drives a Volkswagen Passat which emits 114g/km of CO_2.

(a) What would be the cost of Road Tax for one year for this car?   **1**

(b) If Alan travels to London and back, by car, how much CO_2 would be emitted?

Answer in kilograms, to 3 significant figures.   **4**

(c) If Alan chose the "greenest" method of travel, how much less CO_2 would be emitted for his journey there and back?   **4**

Total marks   9

MARKS

5. Imran is in charge of planning a sailing route in a lake for a sailing competition.

He needs to place buoys as marked on the diagram.

(a) Plan a route he can take, from the "Home Port" to visit all five locations.

He can visit the locations in any order.

The route must start and finish at "Home Port".

Make sure you do not hit the harbour walls!

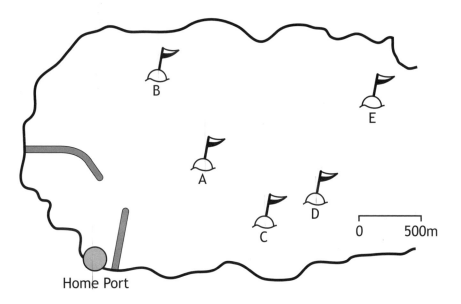

Record a possible route for Imran in a table like this.

4

From	To	Bearing	Distance
Home Port	B	025°	1.5km

MARKS | DO NOT WRITE IN THIS MARGIN

Question 5 (continued)

(b) Calculate the total distance of your suggested route. **4**

Total marks 8

MARKS

DO NOT
WRITE IN
THIS
MARGIN

6. In the Paralympic Games, archers have to shoot at a target 70m away.

    Half a degree in either direction could mean the difference between hitting a bullseye and missing the target completely.

    A diagram of the archery target used at the 2012 London Paralympics is below.

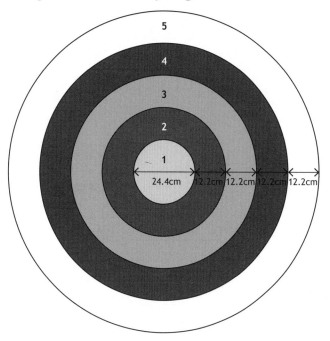

    A diagram of the archery field used in the 2004 Athens Paralympics is below.

    The field is a rectangle with a semi-circular end.

    The field is covered in artificial turf costing €15 per square metre.

    The perimeter of the field is marked out using safety tape.

    Safety tape costs €8.25 for a 10 metre roll.

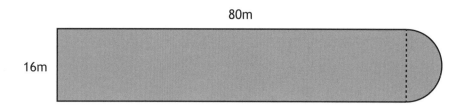

MARKS

Question 6 (continued)

(a) An archer lands an arrow 45cm from the exact centre of the target. In which number ring does the arrow land? **2**

(b) Calculate the area of the central section of the target. **3**

(c) A competitor states that area 3 is more than twice the size of area 2.

Is this statement correct? Use your working to support your answer. **5**

(d) Work out the total cost of the turf and the safety tape.

Give your answer to the nearest euro. **5**

(e) Convert your answer to part (d) into pounds using an exchange rate of £1 = €1.12 **2**

Total marks 17

[END OF MODEL PRACTICE PAPER]

ADDITIONAL SPACE FOR ANSWERS

ADDITIONAL SPACE FOR ANSWERS

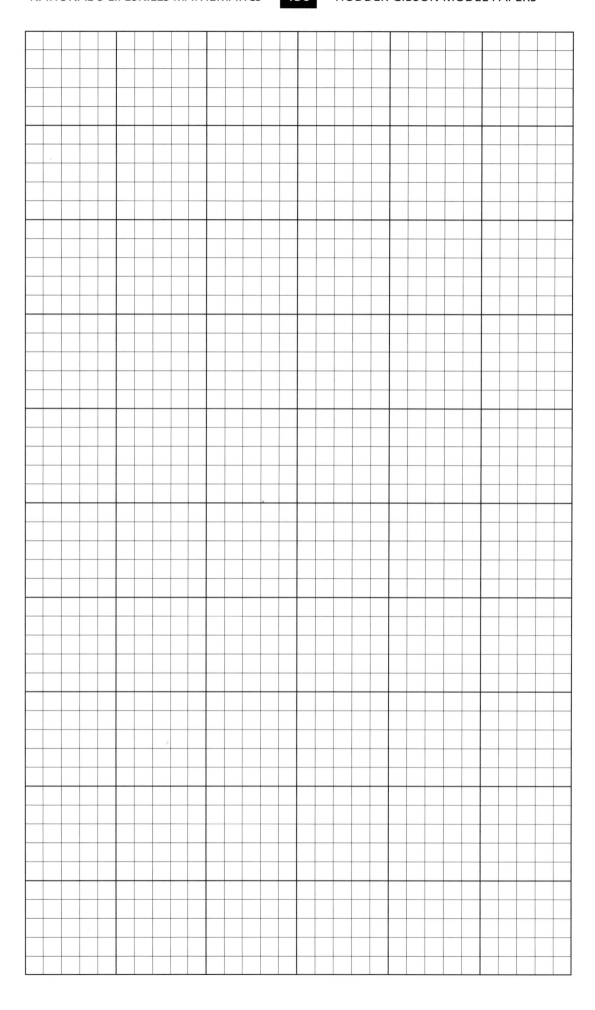

NATIONAL 5

2014

N5

National
Qualifications
2014

Mark

X744/75/01

Lifeskills Mathematics
Paper 1
(Non-Calculator)

FRIDAY, 9 MAY
1:00 PM – 1:50 PM

Fill in these boxes and read what is printed below.

Full name of centre

Town

Forename(s)

Surname

Number of seat

Date of birth
Day   Month   Year

D D   M M   Y Y

Scottish candidate number

Total marks — 35

Attempt ALL questions.

Write your answers in the spaces provided in this booklet. Additional space for answers is provided at the end of this booklet. If you use this space you must clearly identify question number you are attempting.

Use **blue** or **black** ink.

You may NOT use a calculator.

Full credit will be given only to solutions which contain appropriate working.

State the units for your answer where appropriate.

Before leaving the examination room you must give this booklet to the Invigilator; if you do not, you may lose all the marks for this paper.

FORMULAE LIST

Circumference of a circle: $C = \pi d$

Area of a circle: $A = \pi r^2$

Theorem of Pythagoras:

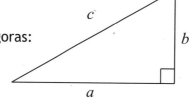

$$a^2 + b^2 = c^2$$

Volume of a cylinder: $V = \pi r^2 h$

Volume of a prism: $V = Ah$

Volume of a cone: $V = \frac{1}{3}\pi r^2 h$

Volume of a sphere: $V = \frac{4}{3}\pi r^3$

Standard deviation: $s = \sqrt{\dfrac{\Sigma(x-\bar{x})^2}{n-1}} = \sqrt{\dfrac{\Sigma x^2 - (\Sigma x)^2/n}{n-1}}$, where n is the sample size.

Gradient:

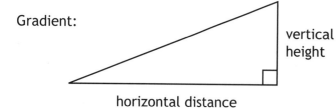

$$\text{Gradient} = \frac{\text{vertical height}}{\text{horizontal distance}}$$

MARKS

DO NOT
WRITE IN
THIS
MARGIN

Attempt ALL questions

1. Mrs Abid took a survey in her mathematics class of how pupils travelled to school.

   The results are shown in the table.

	Walk	Cycle	Bus
Boys	6	4	3
Girls	2	3	12

   What is the probability that a pupil chosen at random is a girl who cycles to school?

   Give your answer in its simplest form.   2

[Turn over

MARKS

DO NOT WRITE IN THIS MARGIN

2. Frances is not feeling well.

She takes her temperature using a thermometer.

Her temperature is shown below.

The temperature of a person in good health is 36·8°C ± 0·4°C.

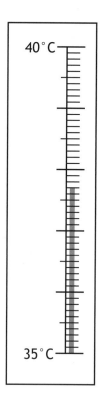

Is Frances in good health?

Give a reason for your answer.

3

MARKS | DO NOT WRITE IN THIS MARGIN

3. A new sail is being designed for a yacht as shown below.

It consists of two right angled triangles.

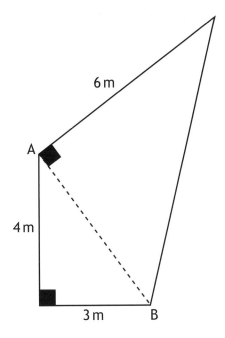

(a) Calculate the length of AB.   1

(b) Calculate the total area of the sail.   2

Total marks   3

[Turn over

MARKS

4. Adam works for 40 hours per week as a tractor driver on a farm.

    His basic wage is £7·40 per hour.

    Each week he pays £28·43 Income Tax and £8·57 in National Insurance.

    (a) Calculate his take home pay.

1

MARKS | DO NOT WRITE IN THIS MARGIN

4. **(continued)**

(b) Adam is going on holiday in 13 weeks.

The holiday costs £320 and Adam wants to take £200 spending money.

He makes a table to show his weekly income and outgoings.

He puts the balance into his holiday fund.

	Income	Outgoings
Take home pay		
Rent		£76
Bills		£41
Food		£45
Entertainment		£30
Transport		£23
Holiday Fund		

Will he have enough to cover the cost of the holiday and his spending money?

Justify your answer. 3

Total marks 4

[Turn over

MARKS | DO NOT WRITE IN THIS MARGIN

5. Reece is given a lift to school.

She leaves the house at 8:30 am and arrives at school at 8:50 am.

She uses an app on her phone to calculate her average speed for the journey.

Her phone displays 6·8m/s.

What distance did she travel?

Give your answer to 2 significant figures.   4

MARKS

6. The Clarks employ Kitease to install a new kitchen for them.

Kitease provide a team of workers to install the kitchen.

The table shows the list of tasks and the time required for each.

Task	Detail	Preceding task	Time(hours)
A	Begin electrics	None	3
B	Build cupboards	None	5
C	Begin plumbing	None	2
D	Plaster walls	A,B,C	8
E	Fit wall cupboards	D	6
F	Fit floor cupboards	D	5
G	Fit worktops	F	3
H	Finish plumbing	G	3
I	Finish electrics	E,G	4

(a) Complete the diagram below by writing these tasks and times in the boxes.

(An additional diagram, if required, can be found on *Page fifteen*.)

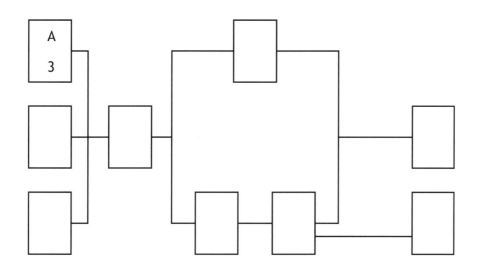

A
3

2

(b) Kitease claim they can install this kitchen in 22 hours.

Is this a valid claim?

Give a reason for your answer.

2

Total marks 4

[Turn over

MARKS | DO NOT WRITE IN THIS MARGIN

7. This back-to-back stem and leaf diagram represents the number of hours a class spends on social networking websites in a week.

```
        Girls |   | Boys
              | 0 | 3 6 8 9
      8 4 3 0 | 1 | 1 2 4 7 7 8 9
9 8 7 6 2 2 1 | 2 | 2 6 7 8 8
        7 2 0 | 3 |
            2 | 4 |
```

n = 15   n = 16

KEY

```
3 | 1 |     represents 13 hours
  | 2 | 5   represents 25 hours
```

(a) A boxplot is drawn to represent one set of data.

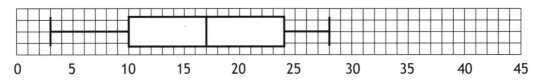

0   5   10   15   20   25   30   35   40   45

Which set of data does this represent?

Give a reason for your answer.   1

MARKS | DO NOT WRITE IN THIS MARGIN

7.   (continued)

(b) For the other set of data, state:

the median

the lower quartile

the upper quartile   2

(c) Construct a box plot for the second set of data.

(An additional diagram, if required, can be found on *Page fifteen*.)

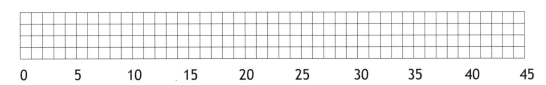

0   5   10   15   20   25   30   35   40   45

2

Total marks   5

[Turn over

MARKS | DO NOT WRITE IN THIS MARGIN

8. Elaine goes on a 5 day long business trip to Oslo in Norway.

    She changes £750 to Norwegian kroner for the trip.

Rates of exchange	
Pounds Sterling (£)	Other Currencies
1	NOK 8·00 (Norwegian kroner)
1	€1·20 (euros)

(a) How many Norwegian kroner will Elaine receive?   1

MARKS | DO NOT WRITE IN THIS MARGIN

8. **(continued)**

(b) Elaine spends NOK 520 each day she is in Norway.

Her company extends her trip by sending her to Munich in Germany for a further 3 days.

If she changes all her remaining kroner to euros, how many euros will she receive?

She spends €135 each day she is in Munich.

How much money does she have left at the end of her trip?

Give your answer in pounds sterling.   5

Total marks   6

[Turn over for Question 9 on *Page Fourteen*

MARKS | DO NOT WRITE IN THIS MARGIN

9. Robbie has a tub for his crayons.

It is in the shape of a pencil as shown below.

It consists of a cylinder with a cone on top.

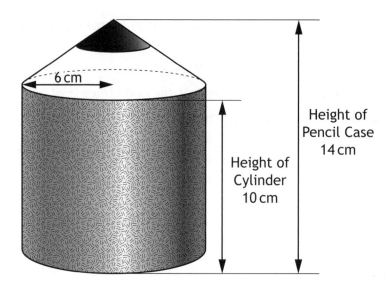

Show that the volume of Robbie's tub is 408π cm^3.

4

[END OF QUESTION PAPER]

MARKS | DO NOT WRITE IN THIS MARGIN

ADDITIONAL SPACE FOR ANSWERS

Additional diagram for Question 6 (a)

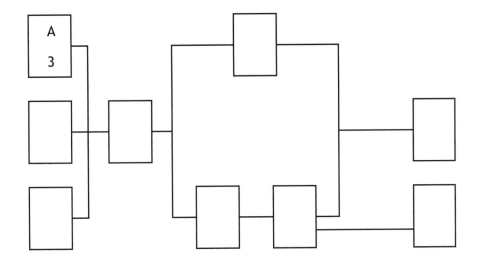

Additional diagram for Question 7 (c)

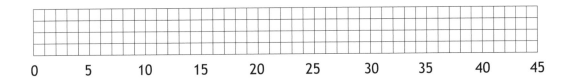

MARKS | DO NOT WRITE IN THIS MARGIN

ADDITIONAL SPACE FOR ANSWERS

N5

National
Qualifications
2014

Mark

X744/75/02

Lifeskills Mathematics
Paper 2

FRIDAY, 9 MAY
2:10 PM – 3:50 PM

Fill in these boxes and read what is printed below.

Full name of centre

Town

Forename(s)

Surname

Number of seat

Date of birth
Day   Month   Year

D D   M M   Y Y

Scottish candidate number

Total marks — 55

Attempt ALL questions.

Write your answers clearly in the spaces provided in this booklet. Additional space for answers is provided at the end of this booklet. If you use this space you must clearly identify the question number you are attempting.

Use **blue** or **black** ink.

You may use a calculator.

Full credit will be given only to solutions which contain appropriate working.

State the units for your answer where appropriate.

Before leaving the examination room you must give this booklet to the Invigilator; if you do not, you may lose all the marks for this paper.

FORMULAE LIST

Circumference of a circle: $C = \pi d$

Area of a circle: $A = \pi r^2$

Theorem of Pythagoras:

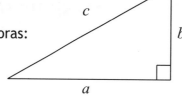

$$a^2 + b^2 = c^2$$

Volume of a cylinder: $V = \pi r^2 h$

Volume of a prism: $V = Ah$

Volume of a cone: $V = \frac{1}{3}\pi r^2 h$

Volume of a sphere: $V = \frac{4}{3}\pi r^3$

Standard deviation: $s = \sqrt{\dfrac{\Sigma(x - \bar{x})^2}{n-1}} = \sqrt{\dfrac{\Sigma x^2 - (\Sigma x)^2/n}{n-1}}$, where n is the sample size.

Gradient:

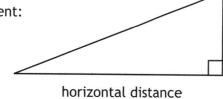

$$\text{gradient} = \frac{\text{vertical height}}{\text{horizontal distance}}$$

MARKS

Attempt ALL questions

1. Over an eight month period, Goran records how much he spends on his pay-as-you-go mobile phone.

£32, £23, £43, £40, £27, £35, £15, £25.

Calculate the mean and standard deviation for this data.   4

[Turn over

MARKS | DO NOT WRITE IN THIS MARGIN

2. The Yellow Jersey Cycle Shop is a retail store that sells items for outdoor activities.

Alan has a 10% discount card for this store.

He receives a flyer showing the store's monthly deals.

He wants to buy all of the following items.

	Mountain Bike Recommended Retail Price £310 Price with discount card £279
	Helmet Recommended Retail Price £20 Price with discount card £18
	Waterproof Jacket Recommended Retail Price £50 Price with discount card £45
	Cycling Shorts Recommended Retail Price £10 Price with discount card £9

Monthly Deal 1	**Monthly Deal 2**
Extra 15% off discounted price when you spend over £75 in store.	Extra 65% off discounted price of bike accessories and clothing when you purchase a bike in store.
Terms & Conditions. 1. Can be used in conjunction with 10% discount card. 2. Not to be used with any other offer or monthly deal. 3. Valid until end of May.	Terms & Conditions. 1. Can be used in conjunction with 10% discount card. 2. Not to be used with any other offer or monthly deal. 3. Valid until end of May.

MARKS

Question 2 (continued)

(a) Which Monthly Deal is better value for Alan?

Justify your answer.   3

(b) After he has bought the items Alan notices the following on his receipt.

> ### The Yellow Jersey Cycle Shop
> ### Price Guarantee
> If any product can be found cheaper (including on special offer) then we will refund the difference plus 10% of the difference.

Alan finds exactly the same items at The Red Polka Dot Cycle Shop who are having a clearance sale.

They are giving 1/3 off the Recommended Retail Price of all the items that Alan has just bought.

How much refund is he entitled to if he uses the **Price Guarantee** from The Yellow Jersey Cycle Shop?   3

Total marks   6

[Turn over

MARKS

DO NOT WRITE IN THIS MARGIN

3. A number of oil rigs operate in the North Sea.

    The map below shows part of the North Sea with the ports of Aberdeen and Ringkobing marked.

    (An additional map, if required, can be found on *Page fourteen*.)

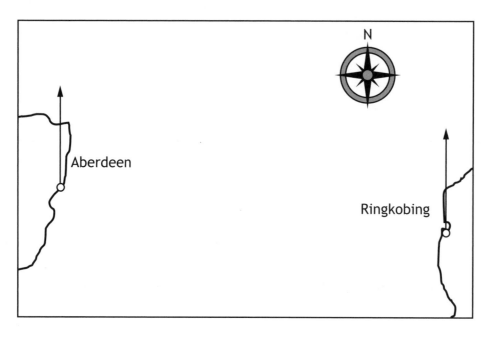

Scale 1 centimetre represents 50 kilometres

(a) Harkins oil rig is 380 km from Aberdeen on a bearing of 065°.

Show the position of the Harkins oil rig on the map above.

2

(b) A fishing vessel issues an SOS call which is received by both ports.

The bearing of the fishing vessel from each port is shown in the table below.

Bearing from	Three figure bearing
Aberdeen	125°
Ringkobing	250°

(i) Mark the position of the fishing vessel on the map.

3

(ii) Find the distance and bearing of the fishing vessel from the oil rig.

2

Total marks   7

MARKS | DO NOT WRITE IN THIS MARGIN

4. Saraish bought her house in May 2009 for £130 000.

In the first two years the value of the house increased by 5% per annum.

For the next three years the value of the house decreased by 2% per annum.

(a) What is the value of the house in May 2014?

Give your answer to the nearest thousand pounds. 5

(b) House prices have risen on average by 4·5% over this five year period.

Has the value of Saraish's house risen in line with this average?

Give a reason for your answer. 2

Total marks 7

[Turn over

MARKS | DO NOT WRITE IN THIS MARGIN

5. A landscape gardener is designing a garden.

The rectangular garden has dimensions 15 metres by 10 metres.

He plans to build a triangular flower bed.

To separate the flower bed from the lawn, he uses a low fence.

The fence is made of 5 sections, each 2·8 metres long.

A patio in the shape of a quarter circle with a radius of 5 metres is to be created in the corner.

The rest of the garden is to be laid as turf.

A sketch of the garden is shown below.

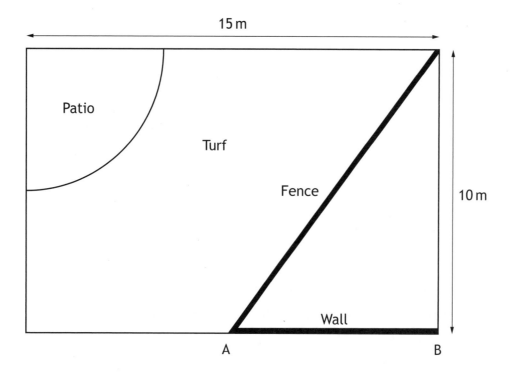

(a) Calculate the length of the wall, AB.

3

MARKS

5. **(continued)**

(b) Turf is sold in $5\,m^2$ rolls costing £14·95 per roll.

Calculate the cost of buying turf for this garden.   6

Total marks   9

[Turn over

MARKS

6. The table shows the qualifying times at the Malaysian 2013 Grand Prix.

    The qualifying times are for 1 lap of the track.

    The track is 5·543 kilometres long.

    There are 56 laps in this Grand Prix.

	Driver	Team	Qualifying Time (min: sec)
1	Sebastian Vettel	Red Bull	01:49·7
2	Felipe Massa	Ferrari	01:50·6
3	Fernando Alonso	Ferrari	01:50·7
4	Lewis Hamilton	Mercedes	01:51·7
5	Mark Webber	Red Bull	01:52·2
6	Nico Rosberg	Mercedes	01:52·5

    (a) Vettel's time was 1 minute 49·7 seconds.

    　　By how much time did Vettel beat Massa?　　　　　　　　　　　1

    (b) What was Lewis Hamilton's average speed in his qualifying lap?

    　　Round your answer to the nearest km/h.　　　　　　　　　　　5

MARKS

6. (continued)

(c) Nico Rosberg's average lap time for the Grand Prix was 1 minute 54·8 seconds.

How long did it take him to complete the Grand Prix?

Give your answer in hours, minutes and seconds.   4

Total marks 10

[Turn over

MARKS | DO NOT WRITE IN THIS MARGIN

7. Cameron wants to resurface his drive.

He has a choice of 3 surfaces.

SURFACE TYPE 1: TARMAC
A tarmac drive should last for 30 years.

Tarmac costs £2 per square foot to lay.

(1 square metre = 10·76 square feet)

SURFACE TYPE 2: GRAVEL CHIPS
A gravel drive should last for 10 years.

Gravel needs to be laid to a depth of 5 cm.

Each 50 kg bag will cover 1 square metre to a depth of 5 cm.
Each 50 kg bag costs £8·29
Each 850 kg bag costs £125·99

The gravel needs a weedproof membrane to be laid underneath.
Membrane to cover the drive costs £14·31.

SURFACE TYPE 3: CONCRETE SLABS
A concrete slab drive should last for 25 years.

Concrete slabs:
40 cm by 40 cm ----------- £2·12 each
Slabs can be cut to size

Slabs require 4 cm depth of hardcore to be laid underneath.
1 cubic metre = 2 tonnes hardcore.
Hardcore costs £18 per tonne bag.

2 bags of mortar at £35·99 per bag.

Cameron makes a sketch of his drive to help him to calculate the cost of each type of surface.

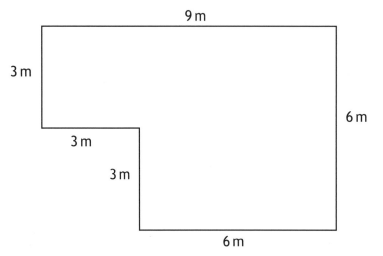

MARKS | DO NOT WRITE IN THIS MARGIN

7. **(continued)**

   (a) Calculate the minimum total cost for each surface type.   **9**

   (b) Which is the most cost effective?   **3**

Total marks 12

[END OF QUESTION PAPER]

MARKS | DO NOT WRITE IN THIS MARGIN

ADDITIONAL SPACE FOR ANSWERS

Additional map for Question 3

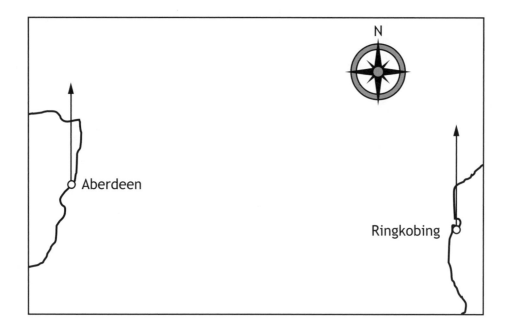

ADDITIONAL SPACE FOR ANSWERS

[BLANK PAGE]

DO NOT WRITE ON THIS PAGE

SQA AND HODDER GIBSON NATIONAL 5 LIFESKILLS MATHEMATICS 2014

NATIONAL 5 LIFESKILLS MATHEMATICS SPECIMEN QUESTION PAPER

Paper 1

1. Elaine has $\frac{35}{56} > \frac{32}{56}$

2. (a) 4 hours

   (b) 63 (mph)

3. £35·50

4. (a) Task letters and times inserted in chart

   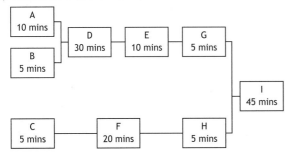

   (b) 100 mins or 1 hr 40 mins

5. (a) All points plotted correctly

   (b) Best fitting line drawn

   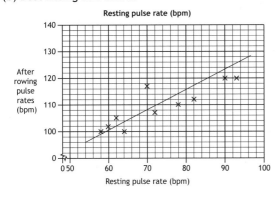

   (c) Rowing, line of best fit is a closer match to pulse rate.

6. 34 euros or 34 (·40) euros

7. 3 : 5 or equivalent

8. (a) £3234 per year

   (b) (i) £535·58
       (ii) £1489·42

9. (a) Yes, the ramp will conform to recommendation 1 because its gradient of 1 in 16 is less steep than 1 in 12.

   (b) Yes, rise is less than 760 mm

10. (a) Appropriate box plot drawn

    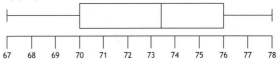

    (b) Any valid comparison for example:
    - Scores tend to be higher in windy conditions
    - There is less spread of data in calm conditions
    - Scores tend to be lower in calm conditions
    - There is a greater spread of scores in windy conditions
    - Scores tend to be more consistent in calm conditions

Paper 2

1. (a) 25·75 (km)

   (b) 65·22 (m/min)

   (c) No, time taken is 24 minutes

2. (a) £68

   (b) Yes, £68 < £91 < 4 × £35

   (c) A family of four unlimited ride wristband is the cheapest

3. (a) (i) $(\bar{x} =)$ 48·7
       (ii) $(s =)$ 1·24

   (b) The athlete's times are slower under the coach. The athlete is more consistent.

   (c) (i) 49·0 (s)
       (ii) 48·0 (s)

   (d) Median, with reason. Reason must refer to the fact that the mean is affected by one very high time or the median is closer to the majority of the times.

4. (a) £2925

   (b) £935·50

   (c) £234

   (d) £6375

   (e) £645

   (f) Yes, store card is cheaper by £334·50

5. (a) 22 pupils

   (b) 8 cm

6. (a) £473·21

   (b) £413

   (c) No, he needs £52·21 more

NATIONAL 5 LIFESKILLS MATHEMATICS MODEL PAPER 1

Paper 1

1. 19.5

2. 17.5 miles

3. 1/18 (accept 2/36)

4. (a) £30

   (b) 12 months (1 year)

5. ShipEasy (cheaper)

6. Type B, mass of tomatoes more consistent

7. 1015pm (2215)

8. (a) Plot points

   (b) Draw line of best fit

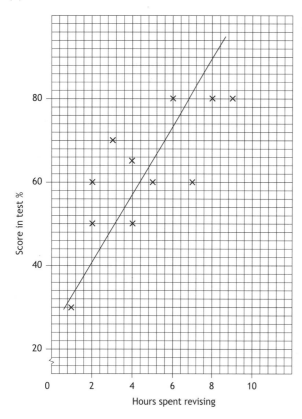

   (c) 4 hours

9. (a) Suitable scale drawing

   (b) 069° (±2°)

10. U bolt, accuracy of 87.5%

Paper 2

1. (a) Box plot drawn

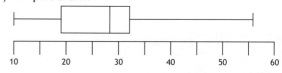

   (b) Kirsten

   (c) More with reason

2. Yes, he reaches a weight of 69.7kg

3. (a) Precedent table and activity network drawn

Activity	Depends on
C	
B	C
A	B C
D	B C
E	D
F	E
G	All

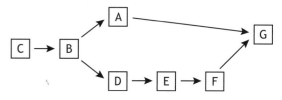

   (b) 10 days

   (c) £1400

4. (a) Accurate scale drawing

   (b) 215 cm (±2cm)

   (c) 1300cm2

   (d) Extra 40 cm

5. (a) 7884.54cm3

   (b) 6100cm3

   (c) 31p (£0.31)

   (d) £2.34

6. Correct completion of table

No. of patients	No. of survivors	Cost for 1 year	No. of patients	No. of survivors	Cost for 1 year	Total No. survivors	Total cost £millions
Treatment B	1 year	£m	Treatment A	1 year	£m		
100	83	3.41	0	0	0	83	£3.41
75	62	2.56	25	15	0.26	77	£2.82
50	42	1.7	50	31	0.52	73	£2.22
25	21	0.85	75	46	0.78	67	£1.63
0	0	0	100	61	1.03	61	£1.03

(a) 75

(b) Correctly drawn graph

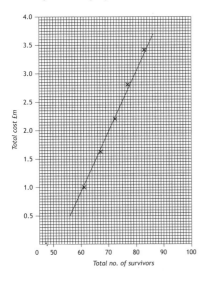

(c) 80 (or from graph)

NATIONAL 5 LIFESKILLS MATHEMATICS MODEL PAPER 2

Paper 1

1. Yes as 180<210

2. No as 1/11>1/12

3. 76 km/hr

4. 148–152mm (14.8–15.2cm)

5. (a) Correctly plotted scattergraph

(b) Line of best fit

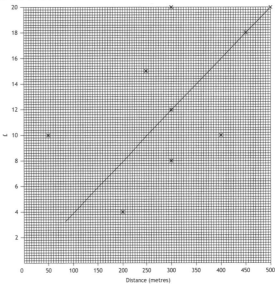

(c) £14 (depends on candidates line of best fit)

6. First option (£12 more pay)

7. 13m

8. (a) 20

(b) 1

9. Correct tasks and times in appropriate boxes and total of 12 hours

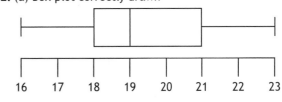

10. 4000, 6000, Manufaturer B
e.g. higher median, slightly less consistent but better IQ range

Paper 2

1. payslip completed correctly

A = £145.92, B = £91.05

C = 236.97, D = £1168.03

2. (a) Box plot correctly drawn

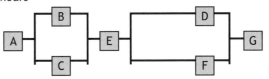

(b) 1/4

3. (a) 0.52cm³

   (b) 0.34cm

   (c) Sphere, 21 spheres can fit but only 20 cylinders

4. (a) (i) 20.5
      (ii) 1.52

   (b) Yes, mean and standard deviation falls within criteria 20.5 is within 0.6 of 20 degrees and 1.52 < 2 for sd

   (c) 9 years

5. (a) 19.2, healthy

   (b) 28.4, overweight

   (c) suitable programme which uses about 500 calories and lasts about 45 minutes

6. (a) accurate scale drawing and total distance given (101km)

   (b) 60%

   (c) 171.5 km²

NATIONAL 5 LIFESKILLS MATHEMATICS MODEL PAPER 3

Paper 1

1. 160 miles

2. £525

3. (a) Surplus (of £25)

   (b) Now deficit of £3

4. (a) Heaviest between 25 and 30 (approx 28kg)

   (b) 16kg

   (c) 17kg

   (d) 60 bags

5. Accurate drawing
   Side = 36m

6. (a) Yes, 20cm × 10cm × 5cm = 1000cm³ = 1 litre and 25cm × 5cm × 8cm = 1000m³ = 1 litre

   (b) First carton (uses less cardboard)

7. (a) Correct completion of table

	9	11	2	5
Mon	M, 9	M, 11	M, 2	M, 5
Tues	T, 9	T, 11	T, 2	T, 5
Wed	W, 9	W, 11	W, 2	W, 5
Thu	Th, 9	Th, 11	Th, 2	Th, 5
Fri	F, 9	F, 11	F, 2	F, 5

   (b) 1/10 (accept 2/20)

8. (a) Min 2.25mm, max 2.35mm

   (b) No, 20% exactly are within tolerance

9. (a) Plot points on scattergraph

   (b) Draw appropriate line of best fit

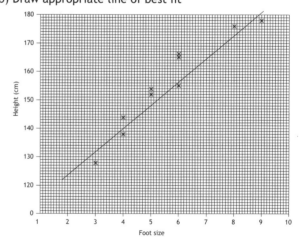

   (c) 165cm (accept ans from graph)

Paper 2

1. (a) 6.6g

   (b) Yes, standard deviation is reduced by 0.8 grams

2. (a) 58600cm³ to 3 sig figs

   (b) Yes, height of ironing box is 29.9 cm

3. (a) Phil (as L=47)

  (b) (i) 58
    (ii) 52
    (iii) 76

  (c) Box plot drawn

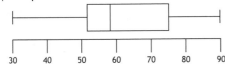

  (d) Rachael's data more spread out or similar

4. (a) Band C £30

  (b) 148kg

  (c) 110.3kg

5. Appropriate route and total distance

6. (a) Ring number 4, the inner edge is 36.6 cm from the centre and the outer edge 48.8 cm

  (b) 467.4 cm²

  (c) Yes with reason

  (d) 20880.45 euros

  (e) £18643.26

NATIONAL 5 LIFESKILLS MATHEMATICS 2014

Paper 1

1. $\frac{1}{10}$

2. No, Frances is not in good health as her temperature (37.7°C) is above the upper tolerance (37.2°C) of good health

3. (a) 5 (m)

  (b) 21 m²

4. (a) £259

  (b) Yes he can afford the holiday as he can save £52 more than he needs

5. 8200 metres (8·2 km)

6. (a) Task letters and times inserted in chart

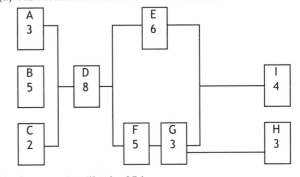

  (b) No, because it will take 25 hours

7. (a) Boys with valid reason

  (b) 26, 18, 30

  (c)

8. (a) NOK 6000

  (b) £87·50

9. Proof

Paper 2

1. (£)30, (£)9·30

2. (a) Monthy Deal 1 is cheaper

  (b) £42·19 (accept £42.18)

3. (a) Mark position

  (b) (i) Mark position
     (ii) 340km, 200°

4. (a) £135 000

  (b) No, value of Saraish's house is about £1000 lower

5. (a) 9·8 metres

  (b) £254·15

6. (a) 0·9s

  (b) 179 (km/hr)

  (c) 1 hour 47 minutes 8·8 seconds

7. (a) £968·40, £357·48, £741·82

  (b) Choice of surface plus reason eg, slabs cheapest per year, or gravel cheaper initially etc

Acknowledgements

Permission has been sought from all relevant copyright holders and Hodder Gibson is grateful for the use of the following:

Image © Umberto Shtanzman/Shutterstock.com (SQP Paper 1 page 3);
Image © Elena Elisseeva/Shutterstock.com (SQP Paper 1 page 4);
Image © Russell Shively/Shutterstock.com (SQP Paper 1 page 6);
Image © Diego Cervo/Shutterstock.com (SQP Paper 1 page 6);
Image © Serghei Starus/Shutterstock.com (SQP Paper 1 page 6);
Image © Steve Cukrov/Shutterstock.com (SQP Paper 1 page 13);
Image © Suzanne Tucker/Shutterstock.com (SQP Paper 2 page 3);
Image © Suzanne Tucker/Shutterstock.com (SQP Paper 2 page 3);
Image © sainthorant daniel/Shutterstock.com (SQP Paper 2 page 3);
Image © Racheal Grazias/Shutterstock.com (SQP Paper 2 page 5);
Image © Maxisport/Shutterstock.com (SQP Paper 2 page 7);
Image © Adriana Muzyliwsky/Shutterstock.com (SQP Paper 2 page 11);
Image © Matthew Cole/Shutterstock.com (SQP Paper 2 page 11);
Image © Samot/Shutterstock.com (SQP Paper 2 page 12);
Image © Abel Tumik/Shutterstock.com (SQP Paper 2 page 12);
Image © Alexander Chaikin/Shutterstock.com (SQP Paper 2 page 12);
With thanks to the Millennium Mathematics Project, University of Cambridge, for giving permission to adapt material from www.maths.org/MathsHealth (Model Paper 1 Paper 2 pages 12–13);
Image © cobalt88/Shutterstock.com (2014 Paper 2 page 3);
Image © hamurishi/Shutterstock.com (2014 Paper 2 page 4);
Image © Photoseeker/Shutterstock.com (2014 Paper 2 page 4);
Image © Aaron Amat/Shutterstock.com (2014 Paper 2 page 4);
Image © nito/Shutterstock.com (2014 Paper 2 page 4).

Hodder Gibson would to thank SQA for use of any past exam questions that may have been used in model papers, whether amended or in original form.